SMOKE
IT LIKE A
PIT MASTER
WITH YOUR
ELECTRIC
SMOKER

SMOKE IT LIKE A PIT MASTER WITH YOUR ELECTRIC SMOKER

Recipes and Techniques for Easy and Delicious BBQ

WENDY O'NEAL

Ulysses Press

Published by
Ulysses Press
P.O. Box 3440
Berkeley, CA 94703
www.ulyssespress.com

ISBN: 978-1-61243-612-8
Library of Congress Catalog Number 2016934502

Printed in Canada by Marquis Book Printing
10 9 8 7 6 5

Acquisitions editor: Casie Vogel
Managing editor: Claire Chun
Project editor: Alice Riegert
Editor: Phyllis Elving
Proofreader: Lauren Harrison
Front cover design: Richard Rossiter
Interior design/layout: what!design @ whatweb.com
Photographs: © Wendy O'Neal except on pages 1 and 135 © Kate Eschbach

Distributed by Publishers Group West

For John, Kaylynn, and Gavin.
I could not have done this without you.
Thank you for inspiring me every day.

CONTENTS

INTRODUCTION

I grew up in a family that loved outdoor cooking. My dad was always firing up the grill for supper, lighting the smoker for weekend parties, and even teaching himself how to cook outdoors with the Dutch oven. When I married, my husband had no idea that we could make such delicious food at home. Sure, he'd had some of my dad's cooking, but most of his experience with barbecue or smoked foods came from chain restaurants.

Shortly after we were married, I bought my husband a $50 charcoal smoker and a smoker cookbook, and he's been in love ever since. We've had cheap smokers, expensive smokers, charcoal smokers, every type of smoker—but my favorite is a good-quality electric smoker. An electric smoker is perfect for hobby cooking. It's easy to use without requiring a lot of fuss during the cooking process.

I'm a self-taught cook, but I was given a great foundation in the kitchen by my mom and my Granny. I remember watching cooking shows on PBS when I'd get home from school and writing down the recipes as the chefs cooked. I loved learning about new cuisines and discovering kitchen tips, so when the Food Network started I was in heaven. I couldn't get enough! I had no desire to become a chef, I just wanted to be able to feed my family good food. The kitchen is the heart of the home and I love bringing family and friends together over a delicious meal.

BECOME YOUR OWN PIT MASTER

My husband claims to be the pit master in our house (shh…we'll let him think that)! He loves getting outside and cooking meat. (I think I've heard him grunt like Tim Allen a few times.) Since outdoor cooking is one of my family's favorite things to do on the weekends, I wanted to write this book to share delicious and easy recipes that anyone can make, whether you're new to electric smoking or have been doing it for years.

The recipes in this book use ingredients that are easy to find, and the techniques involved are uncomplicated. There are tons of great smoking books and resources available for all levels of smoking enthusiasts. This book is for the beginning smoker who already enjoys cooking.

SMOKING VS. GRILLING

Smoking is a low-and-slow cooking process, much different from grilling. Smoking temperatures are usually around 200°F to 275°F, compared to the high heat typically used for grilling (over 400°F). Because smoking uses low heat and the meat is generally farther away from the heat source than it is for grilling, a much longer cooking time is required.

For large cuts of meat, plan on about 1 to 1½ hours of smoking per pound of meat. Cooking times will vary slightly according to the size, shape, and cut of the meat and how often you open the smoker door to check on it.

Of course, smoking isn't just limited to meat—vegetables, breads, desserts, and even cheese are great in the smoker.

Don't Let the Heat Out!

Opening the door lets out heat, and the electric smoker has to come back up to the programmed temperature, which increases cooking time. Avoid opening the door to check on your meat, only doing so if needed.

ELECTRIC VS. CHARCOAL

Over the years I've used both electric and charcoal smokers. While some people swear by charcoal smokers, they take a lot of patience and attention. That was perfect for me when I didn't have kids and could sit around watching the meat cook. Charcoal smokers require a more hands-on approach, and more skills and technique. They are what's used for competition barbecue cooking.

However, for the last fifteen years or so I've used only electric smokers and I have to tell you that I prefer them. It's almost a set-it-and-forget-it sort of cooking, though you still have to add wood chips or baste your meat occasionally. The taste is pretty much the same, because the fact is that it's the wood chips that infuse the meats with flavor, not necessarily the charcoal.

ELECTRIC SMOKER FEATURES

Buying an electric smoker doesn't have to be scary or cost a fortune. There are good-quality electric smokers available for around $200. I've used different brands and models over the years, and I've found Masterbuilt and Char-Broil smokers to be of good quality and affordable. For myself, I prefer a Masterbuilt Digital Electric Smoker. Other well-known brands include Bradley, Smoke Hollow, and Smokehouse.

Electric smokers are vertical smokers that have multiple shelves which allow you to cook a lot of food at once. Get a smoker with the largest cooking capacity that you can afford. That way you'll be able to smoke a ton of food all at once and not be limited by space. Here are some options to consider when purchasing your electric smoker:

Glass Door vs. Solid Door—Glass doors look great on the showroom floor and in pictures online, but my experience is that after a couple of uses, the smoke buildup on the glass is so thick that you can't see through it.

Digital vs. Analog—Both are great. An analog electric smoker has fewer parts to malfunction, but digital allows for setting precise temperatures and cooking times. If a digital smoker is in your future, get one that also has a remote control. That way if the controls on the unit happen to malfunction, you can just use the remote. Plus, you can check temperatures and times from the comfort of your home.

Stands or Legs—These are more of a luxury than a necessity. They do raise the smoker off the ground for easier access and they allow for air circulation under the smoker. Both can be purchased aftermarket if you decide you want them.

Temperature Probe—Again, this isn't necessary, but a good probe will help take the guesswork out of deciding when the food is fully cooked. This item can also be purchased aftermarket.

BEFORE YOU SMOKE

Most electric smokers come fully assembled, unless they have a stand or legs. After you've removed all the packaging and cleaned the racks, trays, and pans with soap and water, you'll need to season the inside before you begin using your smoker.

Seasoning varies according to the brand and model, so refer to your electric smoker's user manual. For my Masterbuilt, the instructions say to heat the smoker to 275°F for 3 hours with a dry water pan in place, adding wood chips once during the last 45 minutes, and then to turn off the smoker and let it cool completely. Some smokers require rubbing a light layer of oil inside the smoker before seasoning it.

CLEANING & MAINTENANCE

Clean the smoker's drip pans and trays after every smoking session, but wait for the smoker to completely cool down first. (I usually wait until the next day, since I generally use my smoker to cook supper. Letting it sit overnight ensures that it's completely cool.)

Empty the drippings from the water pan into a disposable cup, a doubled plastic bag, or anything that can be sealed and thrown into the trash. *Do not* dump the drippings down the sink! Over time this could lead to a seriously clogged drain, which is no fun at all.

After emptying the water pan, remove all the smoker's racks and pans and clean them with regular dishwashing soap and hot water. Let them dry completely and return them to the smoker.

There's usually no need to clean the inside walls of the smoker. The black soot that builds up on them actually gives off a ton of flavor. In all my years of smoking, I've never had to clean the inside of a smoker. However, that doesn't mean there aren't occasions when it might be necessary. In rare circumstances you might need to clean the inside if something was spilled or bugs have gotten in. Don't use any harsh chemicals, but instead use a 50/50 blend of white vinegar and hot water to wipe down the smoker—completely cooled and unplugged—with a soft sponge. The soot will come off the inside walls when you clean them, so you'll need to reseason your smoker.

The best way to keep the outside of your smoker clean is to cover it when it's not in use. Covers can be purchased online, at home improvement stores, or wherever smokers are sold. Having a good cover protects the electronics, too.

ACCESSORIES

In addition to a good cover, there are a few other accessories that are fun and useful to have. Many of these can be found at big box and home improvement stores, online, and anywhere smokers are sold.

Grill Baskets—A few good grill baskets will keep smaller items together and keep food from falling through the slots in the smoker racks.

Disposable Foil Trays—I love using disposable foil trays whenever possible. They come in all shapes and sizes and are usually found in the baking or food storage section of the grocery store. These aren't necessary, but I don't want my good pots and pans to end up covered with a layer of smoke—and disposables make for quick and easy cleanup. An 8 x 12-inch disposable foil pan is the size I use most.

Long-Handled Basting Brushes or Barbecue Mops—The last thing you want to do is to reach your arm to the back of a hot smoker to baste your meat. Long-handled brushes or basting mops are a must!

High-Temperature Gloves—Gloves or heavy-duty potholders are another absolute necessity. The smoker gets extremely hot, and removing food and trays can be tricky.

Cast-Iron Cookware—Cast iron heats evenly and is meant to take the abuse that smoking can inflict on pots and pans. I recommend having a couple different sizes, but measure before buying to make sure they will fit inside your smoker. I suggest having a 10-inch skillet, 8-inch skillet, and a 6- or 8-quart, covered Dutch oven on hand.

Standing Chicken Roaster—A vertical roaster is a fun gadget to keep on hand. You can use it in the smoker, on the grill, or in the oven to cook a bird upright. Most versions have a place where you can add a can to make beer-can or soda-can chicken dinners. Cooking chicken vertically helps to keep it moist and allows the skin to crisp up evenly.

Side Shelf—This great aftermarket add-on provides a convenient place to put your utensils, marinades, and bowl of wood chips.

Slow Smoker—For some smoker models, you can get a slow smoker attachment for the wood chip loading area. This lets you add a large amount of chips all at once, and it will allow a continuous wood feed to provide up to 6 hours of smoke. It's perfect if you can't get out to add chips during a long smoking session.

Shredding Claws—Yes, a pair of forks will work to shred pork or beef, but shredding claws make this task so easy! They are essential for any pit master.

Meat Injector—Many cooks like to inject their meats with liquid solutions to add flavor and keep the meat juicy. You'll need a good-quality injector for recipes that call for this.

Instant Read Thermometer—You'll want a good thermometer for meats that need to be cooked to specific temperatures, such as prime rib and pulled pork. Some heat-resistant models can be inserted for the entire cooking time and will alert you when your meat reaches the target temperature. Others are inserted near the end of the cooking session in order to check the temperature.

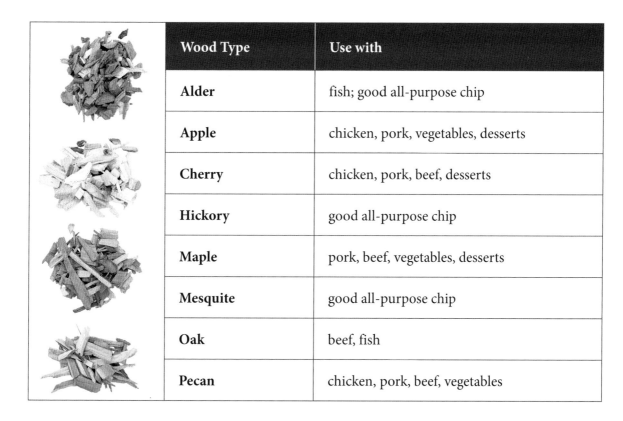

	Wood Type	Use with
	Alder	fish; good all-purpose chip
	Apple	chicken, pork, vegetables, desserts
	Cherry	chicken, pork, beef, desserts
	Hickory	good all-purpose chip
	Maple	pork, beef, vegetables, desserts
	Mesquite	good all-purpose chip
	Oak	beef, fish
	Pecan	chicken, pork, beef, vegetables

WOOD CHIPS

It's a good idea to keep a wide selection of wood chips on hand for your smoker, since different types of wood impart different flavors to food. Pecan, cherry, mesquite, and hickory are some of the kinds used most often. *Mesquite* and *hickory* are great all-purpose woods, while *pecan* is excellent with beef and *cherry* is perfect with pork. I've specified which wood I like to use for each recipe, but if you don't have those chips on hand or if you want to get creative, feel free to switch it up. It's also fun to combine two types of wood chips for a unique flavor.

Plant Ahead!

On a side note, I love smoking so much that when I was buying trees for our yard, I made sure to buy one that I could use for smoking. I ended up buying a mesquite tree so I can dry out the clippings to use in our smoker.

Soaking wood chips makes them burn longer and gives a less intense smoke flavor to food. Dry wood chips burn more quickly and produce a more intense flavor. Both are totally fine—it's a matter of personal preference—though I personally recommend soaking chips for about 30 minutes and then draining a handful before placing them in the smoker, following your smoker's guidelines. Adding wood chips throughout the cooking time imparts wonderful, deep flavor.

If you have unused soaked wood chips at the end of a smoking day, you don't need to toss them. Just dump out the water, let the chips dry completely, and return them to their storage bag.

ELECTRIC SMOKER BASICS

Using an electric smoker is almost as easy as using a slow cooker. Both employ the same low-and-slow cooking method to achieve tender meat. However, the electric smoker is for outdoor use only and should be set up in a well-ventilated area outside, with plenty of open space around it (at least 6 to 12 inches on all sides), directly on cement or dirt.

Before putting anything in to cook, prepare the smoker's water pan (see page 9) unless instructed otherwise for what you're smoking, and turn the smoker on to preheat. This is a good time to start soaking a few handfuls of wood chips in a bowl of water.

After the smoker reaches the desired temperature, place your food inside and close the door. Usually, it doesn't matter which rack you place your food on; however, I typically put the item that will be the messiest closest to the drip pan, so it doesn't drip on anything else that is cooking. Drain a handful of the soaked wood chips and add to the smoker's chip loading area. Keep adding more chips every 30 minutes while your food is cooking (or every 15 minutes for cooking times under an hour), or as specified in the recipe you're using.

An electric smoker has an air damper on top to help control the flow of smoke. For each smoking session, you'll find the sweet spot for how much smoke you like for what you're cooking. A good rule of thumb is to start with the damper halfway open and then adjust as needed. Using the air damper comes with practice and a little trial and error. It takes repeated smoking sessions to decide how much smoke you like. Using too much or too little smoke won't ruin the food, but you'll start to notice if you prefer more or less smokiness to your foods.

7 EASY STEPS FOR SMOKING MEAT

1. Apply a dry or wet rub to the meat, place it in a large zip-top bag or covered dish, and let it marinate in the refrigerator overnight.

2. Add hot tap water to the water pan so that it's about three-quarters full. The amount of water depends on how big your smoker's water pan is; refer to your manufacturer's instructions for best results. (During long smoking sessions, you may need to add more liquid to keep it at that level.) You can also add seasonings, vegetables, or marinades to the water to add flavor during the cooking process.

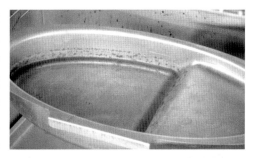

3. Preheat your electric smoker. Once the smoker is hot add food and then a handful of wood chips to the chip loading area. Use the damper on your smoker to adjust the amount of smoke.

4. If you're using a wet rub, pat your meat dry with paper towels before putting it in the smoker. (Any liquid marinades or sauces will burn, so save those for the last 30 minutes.) Place the meat in the smoker, leaving a little room all around to allow air to flow freely, but try to position the meat directly over the water pan so that any drippings will fall into the pan. You'll only need to turn the meat once or twice during the cooking cycle.

5. Maintain the smoker at the desired temperature. Adjusting the damper not only changes the amount of smoke, but can help regulate the temperature. Wood chips can be added as suggested for whatever you're cooking—but keep the door closed as much of the time as possible so that heat doesn't escape, extending the cooking time.

6. During the final 1 to 2 hours, you can baste your meat with a mop sauce or apply your barbecue sauce every 30 minutes.

7. Use a meat thermometer to determine when your meat is cooked to the proper temperature. Once it's at the proper temperature, remove the meat from the smoker and let it rest for 15 to 30 minutes tented loosely with foil to allow the juices to be redistributed, then slice or shred it. Resting applies to most meats; however, fish and seafood are usually served immediately. When you cut into to the meat, you may notice a red ring around the outside. This is the smoke ring and is highly desirable—it doesn't mean the meat is undercooked.

GENERAL SMOKING GUIDELINES

Meat	Smoking Temperature	Time to Complete	Finished Temperature	Wood Chips
Beef brisket	225°F	1½ hrs/pound	190°F (sliced) 200°F (pulled)	Any
Beef ribs	225°F	3–4 hrs	175°F	Pecan
Breakfast sausage	230°F	3 hrs	160°F	Any
Pork butt	225°F	1½ hrs/pound	180°F (sliced) 205°F (pulled) + until tender	Cherry
Pork ribs, baby back	225°F–240°F	5–6 hrs	145°F + until tender	Cherry, Hickory
Whole chicken	250°F	4 hrs	165°F	Mesquite
Whole turkey (12 pounds)	240°F	6½ hrs	165°F	Hickory, Mesquite
Turkey breast (bone-in)	240°F	4–6 hrs	165°F	Hickory, Mesquite
Salmon, steaks, or fillets	140°F–160°F	5–7 hrs	145°F	Hickory
Potatoes	225°F	2–2½ hrs	n/a	Apple, pecan, Hickory

SAFETY

With an electric smoker you don't have an open flame or hot coals to worry about, but there are still safety precautions that need to be taken. Smokers get *hot*, and even the slightest touch can result in a burn. Heavy-duty tongs and potholders are necessities for every grill master. Keep kids and pets away from the electric smoker, as even the outside gets hot.

It's important to protect your smoker from extreme weather (rain, snow, intense sun) in order to safeguard its electronic components. I've had my share of blown fuses at home when the power cord got wet, even when it wasn't in use. I keep my electric smoker under our patio roof, but as close to the edge as possible. This keeps it out of the elements but away from the house, and it provides a quick escape route for the smoke.

Be sure to read your owner's manual for specific details about the electric cooker model that you are using.

FUNDAMENTAL RECIPES

These are my go-to, fundamental recipes. I use them all the time and almost always have a jar of each stored in my pantry or refrigerator. These recipes are the perfect starting point; you can use as a base and put your own spin on them. They're also very forgiving and totally customizable based on your tastes.

TANGY SMOKED BARBECUE SAUCE

The use of whole, smoked tomatoes really gives this barbecue sauce a fresh tomato flavor, while the apple cider vinegar adds a tanginess that you'll love. Since it's made with whole tomatoes, the texture is a little thicker than store-bought sauce, but you'll love it on ribs, brisket, and chicken. Try it on cooked ground beef for scrumptious sloppy joes, and be sure to enjoy the Sweet & Tangy Baby Back Ribs on page 52.

Prep time: 20 minutes   *Marinade time:* None   *Smoking time:* 1½ hours

Wood chips: Pecan

Makes: About 2 cups

4 Roma tomatoes

3 cloves garlic

⅓ cup light brown sugar

¼ cup prepared ketchup

3 tablespoons Basic Barbecue Rub (page 14)

2 tablespoons apple cider vinegar

1 tablespoon Worcestershire sauce

salt and black pepper to taste

1. Prepare the smoker's water pan according to the manufacturer's instructions and preheat the smoker to 215°F. While it heats, fill a medium bowl with water and add 3 or 4 handfuls of pecan wood chips to soak.

2. Place the tomatoes and garlic in a disposable foil pan and set in the smoker. Add a small handful of pecan chips to the chip loading area. Smoke for 1½ hours, adding wood chips at least every 30 minutes.

3. Place the smoked tomatoes and garlic in a medium saucepan, add the remaining ingredients, and bring to a simmer over medium heat on the stovetop. Continue to simmer for 5 to 10 minutes over medium heat, stirring occasionally and breaking up tomatoes. Remove from the heat. Using an immersion blender, countertop blender, or food processor, purée until smooth.

4. The sauce can be used right away or stored in an airtight container in the refrigerator for up to 1 week.

Take Advantage of Space

When I'm smoking vegetables (or whenever I have a little extra room in the smoker), I add the tomatoes and garlic for this sauce. That way I'll have some in the fridge when I'm ready to make more barbecue sauce. The smoked tomatoes and garlic will keep for about a week in the refrigerator.

SMOKED SALT

I always keep a container of smoked salt in my pantry. It's easy to make and is a good filler when there's a little extra room in the smoker. The longer you smoke your salt, the darker and more flavorful it will become. Start with 1 to 1½ hours and go from there. Some of the best salts are smoked for 10 to 15 hours, but those require a lot of care and attention while they're being smoked. Add smoked salt to any recipe that you want to add a little extra flavor, such as grilled meats or vegetables or oven-roasted vegetables, or try rimming a margarita glass with smoked salt for a killer drink.

Prep time: 5 minutes   *Marinade time:* None   *Smoking time:* 1 to 1½ hours

Wood chips: Pecan, mesquite, or hickory

Makes: 2 cups

2 cups coarse kosher salt

1. Preheat your electric smoker to 210°F without using the water pan. While it heats, fill a medium bowl with water and add 3 to 4 handfuls of wood chips to soak.

2. Spread the salt in a disposable foil pan and place in the smoker. Add a small handful of wood chips to the chip loading area, and add more chips at least every 30 minutes. Smoke for 1 to 1½ hours, stirring every 20 to 30 minutes to make sure all the salt gets smoked.

(Feel free to let it smoke longer if you wish. The salt will get darker, and the flavor will be amazing and also a lot stronger.)

3. Remove the pan from the smoker and let the salt cool to room temperature before using or sealing in an airtight container. Store in the pantry for up to 6 months.

Note: If you're adding this to your smoker while smoking something else, don't worry about the type of wood you're using, the temperature, or even the water pan. Just stir the salt every 20 to 30 minutes for a couple hours and it will be fine.

BASIC BARBECUE RUB

This rub is the basis for many of my family's best-loved recipes. It's perfect whether we're smoking or grilling, and not too spicy. I especially love it on ribs, pork shoulder, and even vegetables. This recipe can be doubled or tripled and stored for up to 6 months for easy barbecuing.

Prep time: 5 minutes   *Marinade time:* None   *Smoking time:* None

Wood chips: None

Makes: 1 cup

½ cup light brown sugar

¼ cup plus 1 tablespoon course kosher salt

2 tablespoons garlic powder

1 tablespoon chili powder

1 teaspoon black pepper

1 teaspoon cayenne pepper

1 teaspoon paprika

1 teaspoon dried thyme

1. Combine all the rub ingredients in an airtight container, stirring to mix well. Store in a cool, dark place for up to 6 months.

1 APPETIZERS

SMOKED NUTS

Use these nuts for snacking, on an antipasti platter, in all sorts of recipes from pesto to cookies, or whenever you just want to add a hint of smokiness to something.

Prep time: 5 minutes   *Marinade time:* None   *Smoking time:* 1 to 1½ hours

Wood chips: Maple

Makes: 2 to 3 cups

2 to 3 cups raw, shelled nuts (walnuts, pecans, cashews, or other nuts of your choice)

1. Preheat the smoker to 210°F without using the water pan. While it heats, fill a medium bowl with water and add 3 or 4 handfuls of maple wood chips to soak.

2. Spread the nuts in a disposable 9 x 13-inch foil pan and set in the smoker. Add a small handful of the soaked maple chips to the chip loading area, and keep adding more chips at least every 30 minutes. Stir every 30 minutes until all the nuts are smoked, about 1 to 1½ hours.

3. Remove the pan from the smoker and let the nuts cool to room temperature before serving or using them in a recipe. You can store the smoked nuts in an airtight container for up to 3 weeks.

   Tip: This same technique works to smoke rolled oats for cookies or oatmeal, coconut flakes for cookies and cakes, and even flour for cakes and breads.

   Smoked nuts are great for adding to brownies, cheese platters, sauces, and just general snacking.

POBLANO SALSA

There's something addictive about a good bowl of salsa and a big bag of chips! This Poblano Salsa is delicious with chips and even served better with enchiladas or fajitas. Or offer it as a side dish at lunch with chips and a sandwich.

Prep time: 10 minutes   *Marinade time:* None   *Smoking time:* 1 to 1½ hours

Wood chips: Pecan

Makes: about 2 cups

1 small onion, quartered

4 Roma tomatoes

3 jalapeño chiles

2 cloves garlic

3 poblano chiles

2 limes, juiced, or more as needed

2 teaspoons salt, or more as needed

½ cup chopped fresh cilantro leaves

1. Prepare the smoker's water pan according to the manufacturer's instructions and preheat the smoker to 210°F. While it heats, fill a medium bowl with water and add 3 or 4 handfuls of pecan wood chips to soak.

2. Place the onion, tomatoes, jalapeños, garlic, and poblanos in a disposable foil pan. Set the pan in the smoker and add a small handful of the soaked pecan chips to the chip loading area. Keep adding more chips at least every 30 minutes. Let the vegetables cook for 1 to 1½ hours, or until they are dark and tender.

3. Remove the vegetables from the smoker and let cool. Cut the stems from the chiles and tomatoes and remove the liquid and seeds from the tomatoes. For a less-spicy salsa, seed and devein the chiles; or leave some whole to add spice.

4. Transfer the onion, garlic, and chiles to the bowl of a food processor and pulse to start chopping them. Add the tomatoes, half of the lime juice, and 1 teaspoon of salt and process until the salsa has the desired degree of chunkiness. Add the cilantro and pulse once or twice to incorporate. Taste and adjust the salt and lime level juice as needed.

5. Transfer the salsa to a container with a lid and refrigerate for several hours or overnight to let the flavors combine. The smokiness will mellow as the mixture sits in the refrigerator.

BACON-WRAPPED STUFFED JALAPEÑOS

No day of smoking is complete without including some bacon-wrapped jalapeños! I love the addition of chives and sausage for a fun and flavorful twist.

Prep time: 15 minutes   *Marinade time:* None   *Smoking time:* 40 to 45 minutes

Wood chips: Mesquite

Serves: 10

10 large jalapeño chiles

10 slices thick-cut bacon (about 1 pound)

8 ounces cream cheese, softened

1 pound breakfast sausage, crumbled, cooked, and drained

⅛ cup chopped fresh chives

pinch of salt

1. Preheat the electric smoker to 275°F without using the water pan. While it heats, fill a medium bowl with water and add 3 or 4 handfuls of mesquite wood chips to soak.

2. Cut the jalapeños in half lengthwise, leaving the stems attached but scooping out the seeds and most of the veins. Set aside. Cut the bacon slices in half so that you have 20 short pieces.

3. In a medium bowl, combine the cream cheese, cooked sausage, chives, and salt. Mix well. Working with 2 small spoons, fill a jalapeño half with 1 or 2 spoonfuls of the cream cheese mixture. Wrap a slice of bacon around the stuffed jalapeño, beginning and ending with the bacon ends on the bottom. Repeat with the remaining chiles.

4. Set the jalapeños, filling side up, in a grill basket or disposable foil pan that has been sprayed with cooking spray. Add a small handful of the soaked mesquite chips to the chip loading area and keep adding more chips at least every 15 minutes. Smoke for 40 to 45 minutes, or until the bacon is cooked and crispy.

5. Remove the peppers from the smoker and let cool for 10 minutes before serving. Serve warm or at room temperature.

BEEF JERKY

Store-bought beef jerky is expensive and full of preservatives and salt. Making homemade beef jerky is easy, using ingredients found in most pantries. I always pack some when I'm traveling or when my family goes hiking, but mostly we just like to snack on it.

Prep time: 30 minutes   *Marinade time:* 24 hours   *Smoking time:* 4 to 6 hours

Wood chips: Hickory

Serves: varies

3 pounds boneless beef bottom round

3 cups cold water

1 cup light brown sugar

¼ cup coarse kosher salt

⅛ cup prepared hot sauce

⅛ cup Worcestershire sauce

1 tablespoon garlic powder

1 tablespoon onion powder

2 teaspoons ground coriander

2 teaspoons black pepper

1 teaspoon mustard powder

1 teaspoon dried oregano

1 teaspoon ground sage

½ teaspoon dried thyme

1. Place the beef in the freezer for about 30 minutes to make slicing easier. Then slice it in long, narrow strips about ⅛ to ¼ inch thick (or ask your butcher to do it for you).

2. In a large container or freezer-weight zip-top plastic bag (the 2-gallon size should be just right), gently mix all the remaining ingredients so that the salt and sugar are dissolved. Add the sliced beef, seal, and refrigerate for 24 hours to let the meat marinate. Every few hours, knead the bag or stir in the container to ensure that the beef is evenly coated with marinade.

3. Prepare the smoker's water pan according to the manufacturer's instructions, but substitute about half of the water with the marinade from the meat container. Preheat the smoker to 170°F. (If your smoker doesn't go down to 170°F, set it as low as it will go.) While it heats, fill a medium bowl with water and add a handful of hickory wood chips to soak.

4. Remove the beef strips from the remaining marinade and arrange them on a smoker racks in a single layer, trying to keep them from touching each other. Place a couple handfuls of the soaked hickory chips in the chip loading area. This is the only time you should add chips; otherwise the jerky might turn bitter. Since the meat is so thin, there is no need to turn or flip it during cooking.

5. The jerky will take from 4 to 6 hours to smoke, depending on your smoker's temperature and the water content of the beef. When done, the meat should be dried out but still a little pliable. Let cool completely, then seal in a zip-top plastic bag and store in the refrigerator for up to 2 weeks.

KILLER STUFFED POTATO SKINS

Part potato skin and part twice-baked potatoes, these stuffed potatoes skins make a great appetizer or side dish for any occasion.

Prep time: 20 minutes   *Marinade time:* None   *Smoking time:* 1 hour

Wood chips: Hickory

Serves: 8

4 large russet potatoes

2 tablespoons sour cream, plus more for topping

1 cup shredded Cheddar cheese, plus more for topping

4 slices bacon, cooked and crumbled

4 green onions (whites and greens), finely minced, plus more for topping

½ cup prepared guacamole

salt and black pepper

1. Pierce each potato several times with a fork. Wrap individually in paper towels and cook in the microwave for about 10 to 15 minutes, or until tender. (Alternatively, plan ahead and bake your potatoes in a 425°F oven for 50 minutes to 1 hour directly on the oven rack or a baking sheet. Turn potatoes every 20 minutes during baking.) Set aside to cool.

2. Prepare the smoker's water pan according to the manufacturer's instructions and preheat the smoker to 275°F. While it heats, fill a medium bowl with water and add 2 handfuls of hickory wood chips to soak.

3. When the potatoes are cool enough to handle, cut in half lengthwise and scoop out three-quarters of the insides from each half, leaving about ¼ inch of potato in the skin. In a medium bowl, use a fork to mash the potato flesh you've removed. Add the 2 tablespoons sour cream, 1 cup cheese, and salt and pepper to taste; mix well. Scoop the filling into the potato skins.

4. Top the stuffed potato skins with the crumbled bacon, green onions, and a little more cheese. Place directly on a smoker rack and add a small handful of the soaked hickory chips to the chip loading area. Add chips again after they've been smoking for 30 minutes. Smoke for 1 hour, or until the stuffing is hot and bubbly and the cheese is melted.

5. Top heated potatoes with sour cream, guacamole, and additional chopped green onions as desired.

BARBECUE MEATBALLS

These meatballs make a quick and tasty appetizer for a summer picnic or a winter football party. As a variation, try them wrapping the meatballs in bacon before smoking them.

Prep time: 15 minutes   *Marinade time:* None   *Smoking time:* 1 to 1¼ hours

Wood chips: Hickory

Makes: 15 to 20 meatballs

1 pound ground chicken

¼ cup bread crumbs (either regular or gluten-free)

½ teaspoon salt

½ teaspoon ground cumin

½ teaspoon chili powder

¼ teaspoon black pepper

4 cloves garlic, finely minced

1 tablespoon minced green onions (whites and greens)

¾ cup Tangy Smoked Barbecue Sauce (page 12), divided, plus more for serving if desired

1. Preheat the electric smoker to 275°F without using the water pan. While it heats, fill a medium bowl with water and add 2 handfuls of hickory wood chips to soak.

2. In a large bowl, combine the ground chicken with the next 7 ingredients (bread crumbs through green onions) and ¼ cup of the barbecue sauce. Use your hands to gently mix everything together. The key to a moist and tender meatball is to not overwork it.

3. Using a large cookie scoop (1 to 2-tablespoon size), scoop out some of the chicken mixture and roll it gently into a ball; set aside. Continue forming meatballs with the rest of the mixture.

4. Spray a grill basket with cooking spray and place the meatballs in a single layer in the basket. Add a small handful of the soaked hickory chips to the chip loading area. Add more chips and baste the tops and sides with the remaining ½ cup barbecue sauce at least every 30 minutes. (There is no need to turn the meatballs while they cook.)

5. Smoke until the meatballs are fully cooked, about 1 hour. Serve warm on skewers or toothpicks, and offer more barbecue sauce for dipping, if you wish.

BACON-WRAPPED STUFFED DATES

These single bites of heaven make the perfect potluck dish. Sweet, salty, and easy to assemble at the last minute, they are one of my personal guilty pleasures.

Prep time: 30 minutes   *Marinade time:* None   *Smoking time:* 40 to 45 minutes

Wood chips: Mesquite

Makes: 36 appetizers

4 ounces cream cheese, softened

2 tablespoons finely chopped chives

36 pitted dates

1 pound sliced bacon (or 12 slices), each strip cut into thirds

maple syrup, slightly warmed, for brushing and dipping

36 toothpicks (optional)

1. Preheat the electric smoker to 275°F without using the water pan. While it heats, fill a medium bowl with water and add 3 or 4 handfuls of mesquite wood chips to soak.

2. In a medium bowl, combine the cream cheese and chives, mixing well. Gently slice into a date to separate the halves, without cutting them apart (essentially you are butterflying the date). Working with 2 small spoons, fill the date with a scoop of cream cheese mixture and gently press the halves back together. Wrap a slice of bacon around the stuffed date, beginning and ending with the bacon ends on the bottom; secure with a toothpick if needed. Repeat with the remaining dates.

3. Place the stuffed dates in a grill basket or 8 x 12-inch disposable foil pan that is sprayed with cooking spray and brush with warm maple syrup. Add a small handful of the soaked mesquite chips to the chip loading area. Every 15 minutes, turn over the dates and baste with maple syrup, then add more wood chips. Smoke for 40 to 45 minutes, or until the bacon is cooked and crispy.

4. Remove from the smoker and let cool for 10 minutes before serving. Serve warm or at room temperature, with additional warm maple syrup for dipping.

Note: Please use real maple syrup! The taste is so much better with the real stuff.

SMOKED CHEESE

Including smoked cheese on an appetizer tray or cheese board adds a unique flavor note. Serve this cheese with crackers, smoked nuts, olives, or sun-dried tomatoes. Smoking cheese requires a cold smoking process and a week's wait, but it's worth it!

Prep time: 5 minutes   *Marinade time:* None   *Smoking time:* 1 hour

Wood chips: Pecan

Makes: 1 pound

1 pound Cheddar cheese

1. Preheat the smoker to 190°F without using the water pan.

2. While it heats, cut the cheese into 1-inch slices. Fill a disposable foil pan with ice cubes and cover with a sheet of foil; this will keep the cheese cool enough that it won't melt. Arrange the cheese slices in a single layer on the foil.

3. Set the pan on the top rack of the smoker and add a handful of dry (not soaked) pecan wood chips to the chip loading area. Check the ice level in the pan every 15 minutes, drain any melted water and add more ice as needed to keep the cheese cool. After 30 minutes of smoking, add more dry pecan chips and flip the cheese slices.

4. Remove the pan from the smoker after 1 hour. Transfer the cheese slices onto paper towels to absorb any excess oil. When completely cool, wrap the slices in several clean paper towels and place in a zip-top plastic bag. Refrigerate for 1 week before using to let the cheese mellow. Keep cheese wrapped in clean paper towels in a zip-top bag in the refrigerator for up to two weeks after smoking.

2 POULTRY

BACON-WRAPPED GARLIC SAGE CHICKEN TENDERS

This gets top votes in our household! I make it these chicken tenders on the stovetop and, on the grill, too, but my favorite has to be lightly smoking them with hickory chips.

Prep time: 30 minutes   *Marinade time:* None   *Smoking time:* 1½ to 2 hours

Wood chips: Hickory

Serves: 4

2 pounds chicken tenders (about 6 to 8 tenders)

salt and black pepper

garlic powder

6 to 8 fresh whole sage leaves

6 to 8 slices bacon

FOR THE HONEY MUSTARD POPPY SEED DIPPING SAUCE:

¼ cup yellow mustard

¼ cup honey

½ teaspoon poppy seeds

1. Prepare the smoker's water pan according to the manufacturer's instructions and preheat the smoker to 250°F. While it heats, fill a medium bowl with water and add 3 or 4 handfuls of hickory wood chips to soak.

2. Sprinkle the chicken tenders all over with salt, pepper, and garlic powder, then add 1 sage leaf to the top of each tender. Wrap a slice of bacon around each tender so that the bacon ends are on the bottom (opposite the sage). Carefully place the tenders on the smoker rack, sage side up. Add a small handful of the soaked hickory chips to the chip loading area, and keep adding more chips at least every 30 minutes.

3. While the chicken is smoking, prepare the dipping sauce. In a small bowl, whisk together the mustard, honey, and poppy seeds.

4. The tenders are done when they reach an internal temperature of 165°F and the bacon is crispy, about 1½ to 2 hours. Serve warm with the dipping sauce.

   Note: If the sage leaves are small, then use two small leaves per chicken tender.

SPICED CHICKEN WINGS

Chicken wings are always a hit for parties, holidays, and—of course!—football games. This version is spicy and full of flavor. The thick coating of seasonings helps the skin crisp up in the smoker.

Prep Time: 15 minutes   *Marinade time:* None   *Smoking time:* 1 ½ hours

Wood Chips: Pecan

Serves: 6 to 8

3 pounds chicken wing pieces (thawed if frozen)

1 tablespoon canola or vegetable oil

1 tablespoon light brown sugar

¼ cup coarse kosher salt

2 teaspoons chili powder

2 teaspoons paprika

2 teaspoons garlic powder

2 teaspoons onion powder

2 teaspoons mustard powder

1 teaspoon ground cumin

¾ teaspoon black pepper

¾ teaspoon sage

¾ teaspoon dried thyme

¾ teaspoon dried oregano

½ teaspoon cayenne pepper

prepared ranch dressing and cut-up fresh vegetables, for serving

1. Prepare the smoker's water pan according to the manufacturer's instructions and preheat the smoker to 275°F. While it heats, fill a medium bowl with water and add 3 or 4 handfuls of pecan wood chips to soak.

2. Using paper towels, pat each chicken wing dry (this helps the skin crisp). Place the wings in a large zip-top plastic bag, add the oil, and seal. Roll the wings around in the bag to completely coat them with the oil.

3. Combine the brown sugar and seasonings in a small bowl, stirring to mix well. Add to the bag with the chicken wings, reseal, and move the chicken pieces around in the bag to thickly coat them with the seasoning mixture.

4. Remove the chicken wings from the bag and carefully place them in a single layer directly on a smoker racks. Add a small handful of the soaked pecan chips to the chip loading area, and keep adding more chips at least every 30 minutes. The chicken is done when it reaches an internal temperature of 165°F, about 1½ hours.

5. Serve the wings hot along with ranch dressing and fresh vegetables.

STANDING WHOLE CHICKEN

This chicken will impress everyone—they won't guess how easy it was to make! You just need to have a vertical roaster. Cooking a chicken standing up keeps the whole bird super-moist and lets the skin crisp up all over.

Prep time: 15 minutes   *Marinade time:* None   *Smoking time:* 1½ to 2 hours

Wood chips: Hickory

Serves: 4 to 6

12 cloves garlic, divided

½ onion, quartered

½ lemon, quartered

1 tablespoon salt

1 teaspoon black pepper

1½ tablespoons ground sage

1½ tablespoons dried thyme

1½ tablespoons dried rosemary

1 teaspoon paprika

1 whole chicken (4 to 6 pounds)

3 tablespoons canola or vegetable oil

1. Prepare the smoker's water pan according to the manufacturer's instructions and remove one or two top racks from smoker to make room for the standing chicken. Smash 8 of the garlic cloves and add to the water in the pan along with the onion and lemon pieces. Preheat the smoker to 250°F. While it heats, fill a medium bowl with water and add 3 or 4 handfuls of hickory wood chips to soak.

2. Finely mince the remaining 4 garlic cloves and combine in a small bowl with the salt, pepper, sage, thyme, rosemary, and paprika; set aside. Remove the package of giblets from the cavity of the chicken, then rinse the bird and dry well. Rub with oil and then coat heavily with the seasoning mixture on both the inside and outside of the chicken.

3. Set the chicken on the vertical roaster and place it in the smoker. Add a small handful of the soaked hickory chips to the chip loading area, and keep adding chips at least every 30 minutes. The chicken is done when it reaches an internal temperature of 165°F, about 1½ to 2 hours.

4. Let stand 10 to 15 minutes to cool before removing from the vertical roaster and carving.

BEST DAMN HOLIDAY TURKEY BREAST

Fresh herbs are a must and the butter just melts right into the bird, which makes this the juiciest, most flavorful, and easiest holiday turkey. Guests will want your secret recipe, but you don't have to share it if you don't want to.

Prep Time: 15 minutes   *Marinade time:* None   *Smoking time:* 3½ to 4½ hours

Wood Chips: Cherry, hickory, or apple

Serves: 6 to 8

6 to 8-pound bone-in whole turkey breast

½ cup (1 stick) butter, softened

¼ cup chopped fresh herbs (about 1 tablespoon each of rosemary, thyme, sage, and oregano)

1 tablespoon minced garlic

1 tablespoon coarse kosher salt

1 teaspoon black pepper

1. Prepare the smoker's water pan according to the manufacturer's instructions and preheat the electric smoker to 250°F. While it heats, fill a medium bowl with water and add 3 or 4 handfuls of wood chips to soak.

2. Remove any turkey giblets, if your bird comes with them, then rinse and dry well. In a medium bowl, combine the butter with all the remaining ingredients and stir with a fork to combine. Rub the breast heavily on all sides with the butter-and-seasoning mixture; you'll use most if not all of it. Add some under any loose skin for even more flavor.

3. Set the turkey breast directly on a smoker rack, skin side up, and add a small handful of the soaked wood chips to the chip loading area. Keep adding more chips at least every 30 minutes. The turkey is done when it reaches an internal temperature of 165°F, about 3½ to 4½ hours depending on the size of your turkey breast.

4. Remove from smoker and loosely place a foil tent over the breast to cool for 15 to 30 minutes before slicing.

   Note: If you have a large enough smoker to handle a whole 12 to 14-pound turkey, then double the butter and herbs, garlic, salt, and pepper and prepare as directed above. Increase cooking time to 6 to 8 hours (plan 25 to 30 minutes per pound).

CITRUS CHICKEN FAJITAS

These chicken fajitas rival any that you can get at a restaurant. The marinade is made with lemon, lime, and orange, plus plenty of garlic. The chicken and vegetables are smoked but then finished on the grill to create the perfect fajita filling.

Prep time: 20 minutes   *Marinade time:* 6 hours to overnight   *Smoking time:* 1 hour
Grill time: 25 minutes

Wood chips: Hickory

Serves: 6

½ cup canola or vegetable oil, divided

zest and juice of 1 lemon

zest and juice of 1 orange

zest and juice of 3 limes, divided

3 cloves garlic, smashed

2 tablespoons coarse kosher salt

1 tablespoon Worcestershire sauce

½ tablespoon chili powder

2 teaspoons ground cumin

2 teaspoons black pepper

2 teaspoons onion powder

4 boneless, skinless chicken breast halves (1½ to 2 pounds)

4 bell peppers (any color), seeded

2 onions

4 tablespoons oil, divided

4 green onions (whites and greens), finely minced

¼ cup finely minced fresh cilantro

12 tortillas (corn or flour)

fajita toppings: grated cheese, sour cream, salsa, guacamole

1. In a 1-gallon zip-top plastic bag, combine ¼ cup oil with the zest and juice from the lemon, orange, and 2 limes. Add the garlic, salt, Worcestershire, chili powder, cumin, pepper, and onion powder. Mix well to combine and then add the chicken breasts, turning them in the bag to coat them. Seal the bag and place in the refrigerator to let the chicken marinate for at least 6 hours, or overnight.

2. Prepare the smoker's water pan according to the manufacturer's instructions and preheat the smoker to 275°F. While it heats, fill a medium bowl with water and add 3 or 4 handfuls of hickory wood chips to soak.

3. While the smoker is heating, slice the bell peppers and onions in thin strips and place in a grill basket that has been sprayed with cooking spray. Remove the chicken breasts from their marinade and place directly on a low smoker rack. Place the grill basket with the peppers and onions on the top rack. Add a small handful of the soaked hickory chips to the chip loading area, and add more 30 minutes in. The chicken is done when it reaches an internal temperature of 165°F, about 1 hour. Remove the chicken, onions, and peppers from the smoker and let the chicken rest under a foil tent for 15 to 20 minutes before thinly slicing it.

4. While the chicken is resting, preheat the grill to high heat. Pour 2 tablespoons oil into a large cast-iron skillet and set directly over the heat. Add the smoked onions and peppers and cook until soft and caramelized over high heat, about 15 minutes; stir occasionally to make sure they are caramelizing and not burning. If the onions are burning, lower the temperature to medium or medium-high. Transfer the grilled vegetables to a large bowl. Add 2 more tablespoons oil to the pan on the grill. Add the sliced chicken and allow it to slightly caramelize, stirring occasionally, for about 5 minutes. Return the onions and peppers to the pan for a quick toss with the chicken.

5. Wrap tortillas in foil and place on the grill with indirect heat to gently warm while the chicken cooks on the grill. Flip them once or twice to warm.

6. Remove the pan from the grill. Top the chicken mixture with fresh-squeezed juice from the remaining lime, the green onions, and the cilantro. Serve hot with the tortillas, cheese, sour cream, salsa, and guacamole.

HERBED LEMON CHICKEN THIGHS

Using bone-in thighs keeps this chicken moist. With its fresh lemon flavor, this will become a favorite supper for sure.

Prep time: 15 minutes   *Marinade time:* 1 to 2 hours   *Smoking time:* 2 hours

Wood chips: Pecan

Serves: 4

4 bone-in, skin-on chicken thighs (about 2 pounds total)

zest and juice of 2 lemons

2 tablespoons olive oil

1 tablespoon chopped fresh thyme

1 tablespoon chopped fresh oregano

2 teaspoons salt

1 teaspoon black pepper

1. Place the chicken thighs in a 1-gallon zip-top plastic bag. Add the remaining ingredients, seal, and refrigerate for 1 to 2 hours to let the flavors combine.

2. Prepare the smoker's water pan according to the manufacturer's instructions and preheat the smoker to 225°F. While it heats, fill a medium bowl with water and add 3 or 4 handfuls of pecan wood chips to soak.

3. Remove the chicken pieces from the bag and place them directly on a smoker rack. Add a small handful of the soaked pecan chips to the chip loading area, and keep adding more chips at least every 30 minutes. The chicken is done when it reaches an internal temperature of 165°F, about 2 hours. Remove from the smoker and serve while hot.

CHICKEN & RICE-STUFFED PEPPERS

I love the Mexican flavors in these smoked stuffed peppers. Use leftover taco meat instead of chicken to add even more flavor.

Prep time: 20 minutes   *Marinade time:* None   *Smoking time:* 50 minutes

Wood Chips: Hickory

Serves: 4

4 bell peppers (any color)

½ small onion, finely minced

2 cups cooked rice

1 (10-ounce) can Rotel tomatoes and green chiles

2 cups shredded cooked chicken

2 tablespoons chopped fresh cilantro

salt and black pepper

1. Prepare the smoker's water pan according to the manufacturer's instructions and preheat the smoker to 275°F. While it heats, fill a medium bowl with water and add 1 or 2 handfuls of hickory wood chips to soak.

2. Slice ½ inch off the top of each bell pepper, discarding the stems but saving the rest. Scoop out the membranes and seeds and set the peppers aside.

3. To make the filling, in a large bowl combine the onion, rice, Rotel, chicken, and cilantro. Finely mince the reserved pepper tops and add to the mixture. Season with salt and pepper to taste. Gently spoon the filling into the peppers—no need to press it in firmly.

4. Set the peppers directly on the smoker rack. Add a small handful of the hickory chips to the chip loading area, and add more chips again in 30 minutes. Smoke until the peppers are soft and the filling is heated through, about 50 minutes. Remove and let cool slightly before serving.

SMOKED BUTTER CHICKEN

This classic Indian dish is so delicious, with its complex flavors and unique ingredients. You'll find everything you need at a regular grocery store, but the combination of flavors is out of this world.

Prep time: 30 minutes   *Marinade time:* 1 to 3 hours   *Smoking time:* 1½ hours

Wood chips: Pecan

Serves: 6 to 8

2 pounds boneless, skinless chicken breasts, cut into 1-inch pieces

5 tablespoons butter, divided

1 cup sour cream

1 tablespoon fresh-squeezed lemon juice

2 tablespoons chili powder, divided

2½ tablespoons garam masala, divided

2 tablespoons plus 2 teaspoons minced garlic (about 10 to 12 cloves)

1 tablespoon plus 2 teaspoons freshly grated ginger, divided

2 teaspoons coarse kosher salt, divided

1 medium onion, minced

1 jalapeño chile, seeded and minced

1 tablespoon sugar

1 teaspoon ground coriander

1 (28-ounce) can crushed tomatoes

1 tablespoon tomato paste

¾ cup heavy cream

cooked rice and naan bread, for serving

1. Place the chicken breasts in a 1-gallon zip-top plastic bag. Melt 3 tablespoons of the butter and add to the bag along with the sour cream, lemon juice, 1 tablespoon chili powder, 1 tablespoon garam masala, 2 teaspoons garlic, 2 teaspoons ginger, and 1 teaspoon salt. Seal the bag and gently massage to combine the ingredients. Refrigerate for 1 to 3 hours to marinate the chicken.

2. Prepare the smoker's water pan according to the manufacturer's instructions and preheat the smoker to 250°F. While it heats, fill a medium bowl with water and add 3 or 4 handfuls of pecan wood chips to soak.

3. Pour the chicken and marinade into a 10-inch cast-iron skillet and place in the smoker, but don't add any wood chips yet. Cook for 30 minutes, stirring after 15 minutes.

4. While the chicken is cooking, add the remaining 2 tablespoons butter and 2 tablespoons garlic to a medium skillet along with the onion and jalapeño. Cook on the stovetop over medium-high heat for 3 to 5 minutes, or until the onion is soft and translucent. Stir in the sugar, coriander, and remaining 1 tablespoon chili powder, 1½ tablespoons garam masala, 1 tablespoon ginger, and 1 teaspoon salt. Cook for 1 minute to release the flavors, then stir in the crushed tomatoes, tomato paste, and heavy cream. Bring to a boil, reduce the heat to low, and simmer for 5 minutes, stirring occasionally. Remove from the heat and carefully remove the cast-iron skillet from the smoker. Pour the sauce into the cast-iron skillet with the chicken and stir to combine. Return the cast-iron skillet to the smoker.

5. Close the smoker door and add a handful of the soaked pecan chips to the chip loading area. Add more chips and stir the chicken and sauce again in 30 minutes. The chicken is done when its internal temperature reaches 165°F, about 1 more hour (total cooking time about 1½ hours).

6. Remove the skillet from the smoker and serve the chicken and its sauce over rice, along with Indian naan bread.

3 PORK

SWEET & TANGY BABY BACK RIBS

A little sweet from the brown sugar and a little tangy from the vinegar, these simple baby back ribs are sure to be a crowd-pleaser. A quick trip to the grill adds a crisp finish.

Prep time: 20 minutes   *Marinade time:* 1 hour to overnight   *Smoking time:* 4 to 5 hours
Grill time: 8 minutes

Wood chips: Pecan

Serves: 6 to 8

14 to 16 pounds baby back pork ribs
(about 4 racks)

1 cup Basic Barbecue Rub (page 14)

1 cup Tangy Smoked Barbecue Sauce
(page 12), or sauce of your choice

1. Prepare the ribs by removing the thin membrane from the back side (see page 53). Pat the ribs dry with a paper towel and liberally apply the Basic Barbecue Rub all over, including the ends and side pieces. Place the ribs in a large zip-top plastic bags and refrigerate for at least an hour, or preferably overnight.

2. Prepare the smoker's water pan according to the manufacturer's instructions and preheat the smoker to 225°F. While it heats, fill a medium bowl with water and add 3 or 4 handfuls of pecan wood chips to soak.

3. Use tongs to remove the ribs from their bag and place them directly on the smoker racks, meat side facing up. Add a small handful of the soaked pecan chips to the chip loading area, and keep adding more chips at least every 30 minutes. Smoke the ribs for 4 to 5 hours, until the bones start to show and the meat is tender but not falling off the bone.

4. For a crispy rib, finish the ribs on the grill. Preheat the grill while the ribs finish smoking, then grill over medium heat for just 3 to 4 minutes per side, basting with the barbecue sauce or your own choice of sauce.

5. Let rest for 15 minutes under a foil tent, cut ribs apart to serve, and serve with additional barbecue sauce.

Tip: If your smoker won't hold an entire rack, just cut the ribs into half-rack portions to smoke them.

Removing the Membrane from Your Ribs

Removing the thin membrane from the back side of baby back ribs can be tricky, but it's well worth the effort. Not only does it make the ribs more tender and easier to eat, but it allows the rub and sauce to be absorbed on both sides of the ribs.

Use the tip of a sharp knife to pierce the membrane and begin to separate it from the ribs. Now grab the membrane with a paper towel and pull it away from the entire rack of ribs.

APPLE CIDER BRATS

Instead of making the standard beer-braised brats, use hard apple cider and fresh apples to really change up the flavor of store-bought bratwurst.

Prep time: 20 minutes   *Marinade time:* None   *Smoking time:* 1½ to 2 hours

Wood chips: Apple

Serves: 6 to 8

2 (12-ounce) cans or bottles hard apple cider

1 large red onion, quartered

1 large apple, quartered

6 to 8 fresh bratwurst sausages

6 to 8 large, hearty hot dog buns (optional)

grainy mustard, for serving

FOR THE CARAMELIZED ONIONS AND PEPPERS:

1 tablespoon olive oil

2 white or yellow onions, sliced

2 or 3 large bell peppers (any color), seeded and sliced

1. Prepare the smoker's water pan according to the manufacturer's instructions and preheat the smoker to 250°F. While it heats, fill a medium bowl with water and add 3 or 4 handfuls of apple wood chips to soak.

2. In an 8 x 12-inch disposable foil pan, combine the cider, onion, apple, and sausages. Place in the smoker and add a small handful of the soaked apple wood chips to the chip loading area. Adding more chips at least every 30 minutes, cook the brats until they've reached an internal temperature of 160°F, about 1½ to 2 hours.

3. While the sausages cook, heat the olive oil in a large skillet on the stovetop over medium-high heat for 30 seconds to a minute. Add the sliced onions and peppers and let them caramelize, stirring frequently over medium-high heat to keep them from burning. They are done when soft and lightly browned, about 10 to 15 minutes.

4. Take the brat pan out of the smoker and use tongs to remove the brats from the cider. Serve immediately, with or without buns, topped with the caramelized onions and peppers and the mustard.

HERB-CRUSTED PORK LOIN

Pork loin gets a delicious makeover in the smoker. It's great for a weeknight supper but fancy enough for a dinner party, too. I like to serve applesauce and smoked vegetables alongside the pork.

Prep time: 15 minutes   *Marinade time:* None   *Smoking time:* 2½ to 3 hours

Wood chips: Mesquite

Serves: 6 to 8

3 pounds pork tenderloin

10 cloves garlic

salt and black pepper

½ cup Dijon mustard

½ cup chopped fresh rosemary

FOR THE SWEET MUSTARD SAUCE:

2 tablespoons Dijon mustard

2 tablespoons light brown sugar

½ tablespoon apple cider vinegar

½ cup vegetable or chicken stock or broth

2 teaspoons cornstarch

⅓ cup water

salt

1. Prepare the smoker's water pan according to the manufacturer's instructions and preheat the smoker to 250°F. While it heats, fill a medium bowl with water and add 3 or 4 handfuls of mesquite wood chips to soak.

2. Prepare the tenderloin by poking 10 holes in the meat with a sharp knife all over the tenderloin and stuffing each hole with a clove of garlic. Season with salt and pepper before rubbing Dijon mustard over the entire tenderloin, making sure to coat all surfaces. Then press the chopped rosemary over the whole tenderloin, gently pressing it into the mustard to make sure it stays on.

3. Place the tenderloin directly on the smoker rack and add a small handful of the soaked mesquite chips to the chip loading area. Adding more chips at least every 30 minutes, cook the tenderloin until the internal temperature has reached 155°F, about 2½ to 3 hours.

4. While the tenderloin is cooking, prepare the sauce. In a medium saucepan, combine the mustard, brown sugar, vinegar, and stock. Bring to a boil on the stovetop over medium-high heat, then reduce heat and let simmer for 5 minutes. Meanwhile, in a small bowl stir together the cornstarch and water; slowly pour and whisk into the mustard sauce, which should thicken the mustard sauce almost immediately. Remove the sauce from the heat and season to taste with salt.

5. Let the tenderloin rest under a foil tent for 15 to 20 minutes before slicing. Spoon the sauce over the top to serve.

GLAZED EASTER HAM

Pick up any spiral-cut ham from the grocery store and baste it with this sweet glaze for an Easter ham that's finger-licking good.

Prep time: 15 minutes   *Marinade time:* None   *Smoking time:* 2 hours

Wood chips: Hickory

Serves: 8 to 10

10-pound bone-in spiral-cut ham

½ cup canned pineapple juice

¼ cup light brown sugar

1 tablespoon Worcestershire sauce

½ teaspoon coarse kosher salt

¼ teaspoon ground cloves

¼ teaspoon ground nutmeg

1 teaspoon cornstarch

¼ cup water

1. Prepare the smoker's water pan according to the manufacturer's instructions and preheat the smoker to 275°F. While it heats, fill a medium bowl with water and add 3 or 4 handfuls of hickory wood chips to soak.

2. Place the ham directly on a smoker rack and add a handful of the soaked hickory chips to the chip loading area. While the ham starts to smoke, prepare the glaze. In a small saucepan, combine the pineapple juice, brown sugar, Worcestershire, salt, cloves, and nutmeg. Heat on the stovetop over medium heat, stirring until the sugar is dissolved and the glaze begins to boil. Combine the cornstarch and water in a small bowl, mixing well, and slowly pour into the boiling liquid while whisking to break up any clumps. Let the mixture return to a boil for about a minute and then remove from the heat. Reserve half the glaze for serving.

3. Baste the ham with the glaze and add more wood chips at least every 30 minutes. The ham is already fully cooked, but it will be warm through when it reaches an internal temperature of 140°F, after about 2 hours of smoking.

4. Let the ham cool slightly before slicing. Serve warm along with the remaining glaze on the side, if desired.

PULLED PORK SANDWICHES

Pulled pork sounds easy, but it can be hard to get it just right. The key to juicy, tender pulled pork is the length of time it cooks. Smoke it low and slow for the moistest, tenderest pulled pork you'll ever have. A side of coleslaw is traditional.

Prep time: 15 minutes   *Marinade time:* 4 hours to overnight   *Smoking time:* 8 to 10 hours

Wood chips: Hickory

Serves: 8 to 10

1 (7-pound) boneless pork butt

¾ to 1 cup plus 2 tablespoons Basic Barbecue Rub (page 14)

1 cup water

½ cup apple cider vinegar

1 (½-inch) onion slice

2 lemon slices

hamburger buns, for serving

1. Prepare the smoker's water pan according to the manufacturer's instructions and preheat the smoker to 230°F. While it heats, fill a medium bowl with water and add 5 or 6 handfuls of hickory wood chips to soak.

2. Remove the pork butt from its packaging and dry it with paper towels. Rub ¾ to 1 cup of the Basic Barbecue Rub over the pork so that the entire surface is heavily covered.

3. In a medium bowl, combine the water, vinegar, 2 tablespoons rub, onion, and lemon. Mix well. Put half in a small container with a lid and refrigerate until after the meat is cooked. The rest will be used to baste the meat.

4. Place the pork butt in the smoker and add a small handful of the soaked hickory chips to the chip loading area. Add more chips at least every 30 minutes, and baste the meat with the sauce mixture every 30 to 45 minutes. Smoke for 8 to 10 hours, or until the internal temperature is 165°F. The pork butt might reach that temperature before 8 to 10 hours, but keep cooking to ensure tender meat for pulling. The meat will pull apart easily when it's done.

5. Remove the pork from the smoker and let it cool under a foil tent for about 30 minutes, or until it is cool enough to handle. (It should still be somewhat hot so that it will pull easily). Use a pair of heavy-duty forks to pull the meat into small chunks.

6. While the meat is cooling, remove the reserved sauce from the refrigerator. Strain and gently heat it in a small saucepan on the stovetop. Add to the pulled pork and serve on buns.

Notes: When you're making pulled pork, a good general guideline is to plan on 1½ hours of smoking time per pound.

CRISPY ASIAN BABY BACK RIBS

For a unique spin on a classic, replace barbecue sauce with soy sauce and Chinese five-spice. Throw the ribs onto a hot grill after they've finished cooking in the smoker for a crispy finish.

Prep time: 20 minutes   *Marinade time:* 4 hours to overnight   *Smoking time:* 4 to 5 hours
Grill time: 8 minutes

Wood chips: Pecan

Serves: 4

1 cup light brown sugar

¼ cup Chinese five-spice

8 pounds (or 2 racks) baby back pork ribs

⅓ cup soy sauce or tamari

1. In a small bowl, combine the brown sugar and Chinese five-spice; set aside. Prepare the ribs by removing the thin membrane on the back side (see page 53). Pat the ribs dry with a paper towel.

2. Place in a large zip-top plastic bag and pour in the soy sauce, turning the bag several times to completely coat the ribs. Add the brown sugar mixture, seal the bag, and turn to completely coat the ribs. Seal the bag and refrigerate for several hours, or overnight.

3. Prepare the smoker's water pan according to the manufacturer's instructions and preheat the electric smoker to 225°F. While it heats, fill a medium bowl with water and add 3 or 4 handfuls of pecan wood chips to soak.

4. Using tongs, place the ribs in the smoker with the meat side facing up. Add a small handful of the soaked pecan chips to the chip loading area, and keep adding more chips at least every 30 minutes (or every 15 minutes, for a more intense smoke flavor). Smoke the ribs for 4 to 5 hours, until the bones start to show and the meat is tender but not falling off the bone.

5. For crispy ribs, preheat a grill while the ribs finish cooking. Grill the ribs over medium heat for just 3 to 4 minutes per side.

6. Let rest for 15 minutes under a foil tent and cut the ribs apart to serve.

    Notes: If your smoker won't hold an entire rack of ribs, just cut them into half-rack portions to smoke them.

COLA SPARERIBS

My family asks for these ribs every couple of weeks. Something magic happens when you add a can of Coke to barbecue sauce and ribs. Everything gets a dark, sweet flavor that can only come from that can of soda.

Prep time: 30 minutes   *Marinade time:* 1 hour to overnight   *Smoking time:* 5 to 6 hours

Wood chips: Pecan or hickory

Serves: 6 to 8

2 racks pork spareribs (6 to 8 pounds)

¼ to ½ cup Basic Barbecue Rub (page 14)

FOR THE SAUCE:

1 (12-ounce) can Coca-Cola

2 cups prepared ketchup

2 tablespoons apple cider vinegar

¼ cup light brown sugar

2 tablespoons Basic Barbecue Rub (page 14)

2 cloves garlic, finely minced

1. Prepare the spareribs by removing the thin membrane on the back side (see page 53). Pat the ribs dry with a paper towel and then liberally apply barbecue rub all over, including the ends and side pieces. Place the ribs in a large zip-top plastic bag and refrigerate for at least an hour, or overnight.

2. Prepare the smoker's water pan according to the manufacturer's instructions and preheat the smoker to 225°F. While it heats, fill a medium bowl with water and add 3 or 4 handfuls of wood chips to soak.

3. Using tongs, place the ribs on the smoker racks with the meat side facing up. Add a small handful of the soaked wood chips to the chip loading area, and keep adding more chips at least every 30 minutes.

4. While the ribs are cooking, combine the sauce ingredients in a medium saucepan. Heat on the stovetop over medium heat until sugar has dissolved and then reduce heat and simmer for about 15 minutes, stirring occasionally. The sauce will thicken slightly as it cooks.

5. Smoke the ribs for 5 to 6 hours, basting them with the sauce several times during the last hour of cooking. The ribs are done when the bones start to show and the meat is tender but not falling off the bone. Let rest for 15 minutes under a foil tent, cut the ribs apart to serve, and serve with additional sauce on the side.

HAM STEAKS WITH PINEAPPLE SALSA

Talk about an easy supper! Ham steaks are what I reach for when I need a quick and easy meal. Suppers that are ready in under 30 minutes are always a good thing, and this Pineapple Salsa is amazing. It's good by itself with chips and even better piled high on a smoked ham steak.

Prep time: 15 minutes   *Marinade time:* None   *Smoking time:* 30 minutes

Wood chips: Pecan or hickory

Serves: 6 to 8

2 (1 to 1½-pound) ham steaks

1 cup diced fresh pineapple

½ cup diced red onion

1 jalapeño chile, seeded and diced

1 tablespoon chopped fresh cilantro

½ lime, juiced

pinch of salt

1. Prepare the smoker's water pan according to the manufacturer's instructions and preheat the smoker to 220°F. While it heats, fill a medium bowl with water and add a handful of wood chips to soak.

2. Using tongs, arrange the ham steaks directly on the smoker racks. Add the handful of soaked wood chips to the chip loading area; this is the only time that you'll add chips.

3. While the ham smokes, in a small bowl combine the pineapple, red onion, jalapeño, cilantro, lime juice, and salt; set aside. When the ham has been smoking for about 30 minutes, transfer the warm steaks to a serving platter. Top with the pineapple salsa to serve.

4 BEEF

SIMPLE BRISKET

This is my go-to recipe when I have a craving for brisket but didn't plan ahead. The ingredients are typical pantry staples, making this a quick recipe to throw together.

Prep time: 10 minutes   *Marinade time:* None   *Smoking time:* 4 to 6 hours
Wood chips: Hickory or mesquite
Serves: 10 to 12

4 pounds beef brisket, fat trimmed

2 tablespoons coarse kosher salt

2 tablespoons garlic powder

1 tablespoon black pepper

1 cup Tangy Smoked Barbecue Sauce (page 12)

½ cup Worcestershire sauce

½ cup water

1. Prepare the smoker's water pan according to the manufacturer's instructions and preheat the smoker to 225°F. While it heats, fill a medium bowl with water and add 3 or 4 handfuls of wood chips to soak.

2. Remove the brisket from its wrapping, dry with paper towels, and set aside. In a small bowl, combine the salt, garlic powder, and pepper. Rub the mixture over the brisket, making sure to cover everything heavily.

3. In a medium bowl, combine the barbecue sauce, Worcestershire, and water; mix well. Pour half into a small container with a lid and refrigerate until after the meat is cooked. The remainder will be used to baste the meat.

4. Place the brisket in the smoker, fatty side up, and add a small handful of the soaked wood chips to the chip loading area. Add more chips at least every 30 minutes, and also baste the meat with the sauce mixture every 30 minutes. Smoke for 4 to 6 hours, or until the internal temperature of the meat is 165°F.

5. Remove the brisket from the smoker, wrap tightly in foil, and let rest for 30 minutes. Meanwhile, gently warm the reserved sauce mixture in a small saucepan on the stovetop. Cut the meat into thick slices and serve along with the sauce, or chop up the meat with the sauce.

CLASSIC TEXAS BRISKET

I was born and raised a Texas girl, and Texas barbecue is my number one foodie love. This brisket is smoked for hours and then finished in a foil wrap with lots of delicious barbecue sauce, resulting in an ultra-tender and flavorful brisket.

Prep time: 15 minutes *Marinade time:* None *Smoking time:* 6 to 8 hours

Wood chips: Pecan

Serves: 4

4 pounds beef brisket, fat trimmed

2 tablespoons coarse kosher salt

2 tablespoons garlic powder

2 tablespoons onion powder

2 tablespoons celery powder

1 tablespoon ground cumin

1½ cups Tangy Smoked Barbecue Sauce (page 12), divided

1. Prepare the smoker's water pan according to the manufacturer's instructions and preheat the smoker to 225°F. While it heats, fill a medium bowl with water and add 5 or 6 handfuls of pecan wood chips to soak.

2. Remove the brisket from its packing, dry with paper towels, and set aside. In a small bowl, combine the seasonings (salt through cumin). Rub this mixture over the brisket to cover all surfaces heavily.

3. Place the brisket in the smoker, fatty side up, and add a small handful of the soaked pecan chips to the chip loading area. Keep adding more chips every 30 minutes. At about the 4-hour mark, remove the meat from the smoker and place it on a piece of foil. Pour half the barbecue sauce over the top and then wrap it tightly in foil before returning it to the smoker. There's no need to keep adding wood chips at this point unless you are also smoking something else. Smoke for a total of 6 to 8 hours, or until the meat is tender and has reached an internal temperature of 165°F.

4. Remove the brisket from the smoker and let it rest in the foil for 30 minutes before serving. Cut in thick slices or chop with reserved sauce that's been gently warmed.

GARLIC PEPPER STEAKS

My family's favorite supper is grilled steak with asparagus, and I bet they'd eat it every day if I'd let them. This smoked steak has been a welcome addition to the steak rotation in our household. A fast sear on the grill seals in the juices before the steaks go into the smoker.

Prep time: 5 minutes   *Marinade time:* None   *Smoking time:* 1¼ to 2 hours

Grill time: 2 minutes

Wood chips: Pecan

Serves: 4

2 tablespoons coarse kosher salt

4 teaspoons dried dill weed

4 teaspoons coarsely ground black pepper

4 teaspoons coarsely ground coriander seeds

2 teaspoons garlic powder

2 teaspoons paprika

1 to 2 teaspoons red pepper flakes

4 (6-ounce) rib-eye steaks

6 cloves garlic, finely minced

½ cup (1 stick) butter

1. In a small bowl, combine the salt, dill weed, black pepper, coriander, garlic powder, paprika, and red pepper flakes. Sprinkle 1 to 2 teaspoons of this rub mixture on all sides of each steak. (Store any leftover seasoning in an airtight container for up to 6 months.)

2. Prepare the smoker's water pan according to the manufacturer's instructions and preheat the smoker to 250°F. While it heats, fill a medium bowl with water and add 3 or 4 handfuls of pecan wood chips to soak.

3. Heat a grill to high and sear the steaks for 1 minute on each side, then place them directly on a smoker rack. Add a small handful of the soaked pecan chips to the chip loading area.

4. In a small saucepan, gently warm the minced garlic and butter until melted. Alternatively, heat the garlic and butter in the microwave for 20 to 30 seconds in a microwave-safe bowl. Stir to combine. Every 30 minutes, baste the steaks with the garlic butter and add more wood chips. Smoke the steaks for 1¼ to 2 hours, or until they are done the way you like them. For a medium steak, cook to an internal temperature of 155°F.

BULGOGI

My husband travels the world for his work and always tries exotic new dishes when he travels. He fell in love with bulgogi on a trip to Korea many years ago. Bulgogi is Korean barbecue, and it's usually cooked on the grill. I came up with this smoked version with my husband's help a few years ago, and now it's the only way we make it. The grill still comes into play though, for a quick finish after the steak has been smoked.

Prep time: 5 minutes   *Marinade time:* 6 hours to overnight   *Smoking time:* 1 hour
Grill time: 5 to 10 minutes

Wood chips: Hickory

Serves: 4

1 pound flank steak

⅓ cup soy sauce or tamari

3 tablespoons sugar

6 garlic cloves, finely minced

⅛ teaspoon black pepper

1 teaspoon grated fresh ginger

1 tablespoon mirin or seasoned rice wine vinegar

2 tablespoons canola or vegetable oil

cooked rice

sliced green onions (optional)

sesame seeds (optional)

1. Place the steak in a 1-gallon zip-top plastic bag. Add the soy sauce, sugar, garlic, pepper, ginger, and mirin and mix well to combine. Seal the bag and place in the fridge for at least 6 hours, or overnight.

2. Prepare the smoker's water pan according to the manufacturer's instructions and preheat the smoker to 275°F. While it heats, fill a medium bowl with water and add 3 or 4 handfuls of hickory wood chips to soak.

3. Remove the steak from the marinade and place directly on one of the lower smoker racks. Add a small handful of the soaked hickory chips to the chip loading area, and keep adding more wood chips at least every 30 minutes. The steak is done when it reaches an internal temperature of 150° to 155 °F, about 1 hour. Remove from the smoker and let rest under a foil tent for 10 minutes before thinly slicing the meat against the grain.

4. While the steaks rests, heat your grill to high. Set a large cast-iron skillet directly over the heat and add 2 tablespoons oil. Add the steak slices and heat for about 5 minutes, stirring occasionally, until they become slightly caramelized. Remove from the grill and serve the bulgogi over rice, topped with a sprinkling of sesame seeds and green onions, if desired.

PRIME RIB

Every Christmas, I make this smoked prime rib, and it's the first thing devoured at supper. Just a simple rub and lots of smoke gives you a delicious holiday meal. Finishing the roast on the grill adds a crisp crust.

Prep time: 10 minutes   *Marinade time:* 1 to 2 hours   *Smoking time:* 1½ to 2½ hours   *Grill time:* 12 to 16 minutes

Wood chips: Cherry

Serves: 6 to 8

¼ cup whole peppercorns

¼ cup coarse kosher salt

¼ cup minced garlic (about 20 cloves)

1 tablespoon olive oil

7 to 8-pound boneless beef prime rib roast

1. Grind or smash the peppercorns until coarsely ground, using a coffee grinder, a heavy-duty blender, or even a rolling pin. This will add a nice crust to the outside of your prime rib. In a small bowl, combine the ground peppercorns, salt, and garlic.

2. Rub the olive oil on the roast and then rub the pepper mixture all over the meat. It will be very thick (you'll use all of it) and should cover the entire roast. Place the pepper-coated roast on a plate and cover with plastic wrap and refrigerate for 1 to 2 hours.

3. Prepare the smoker's water pan according to the manufacturer's instructions and preheat the electric smoker to 250°F. While it heats, fill a medium bowl with water and add 3 or 4 handfuls of cherry wood chips to soak.

4. When the smoker is ready, place the prime rib directly on a smoker rack and add a small handful of the soaked cherry wood chips to the chip loading area. Keep adding chips at least every 30 minutes. Use a meat thermometer to monitor the temperature of the roast, and remove it from the smoker when it is about 15°F under the recommended temperature for the degree of doneness you want. Prime rib takes anywhere from 1½ to 2½ hours, depending on whether you like yours rare, medium-rare, or medium.

5. When the meat is close to being ready to take out of the smoker, heat your outdoor grill as hot as it will allow. Transfer the roast to the hot grill and let the outside crust crisp for 3 to 4 minutes per side. After the quick grill, let the meat rest for 15 to 20 minutes under a loose foil tent to finish cooking and allow the juices to be absorbed back into the meat.

6. Cut and serve in ½-inch thick slices with horseradish sauce, if desired.

Temperature Guide

Rare prime rib is done at 125°F to 130°F

Medium-rare prime rib is done at 135°F

Medium prime rib is done at 140°F

BARBECUE MEATLOAF

I'm not the biggest fan of meatloaf, but my family is. I was desperate to find a meatloaf that we'd all love, and this is it. The fat drains away, while the smoke adds a unique flavor that you can't get in traditional baked meatloaf.

Prep time: 20 minutes   *Marinade time:* None   *Smoking time:* 2 to 2½ hours

Wood chips: Cherry

Serves: 4 to 6

1½ pounds lean ground beef

1 cup Tangy Smoked Barbecue Sauce (page 12), divided

¾ cup quick-cooking rolled oats

1 large egg

¼ cup finely minced onion

2 teaspoons Basic Barbecue Rub (page 14)

1. Prepare the smoker's water pan according to the manufacturer's instructions and preheat the smoker to 225°F. While it heats, fill a medium bowl with water and add 3 or 4 handfuls of cherry wood chips to soak.

2. In a large bowl, combine the ground beef, ¾ cup barbecue sauce, oats, egg, onion, and rub. Mix with your hands just until combined, then transfer onto a piece of parchment paper and form into a large log shaped like a bread pan. Spread the remaining ¼ cup barbecue sauce over the top of the meatloaf.

3. Place the meatloaf—on the parchment paper—directly on a smoker rack. Add a small handful of the soaked cherry chips to the chip loading area, and keep adding more chips at least every 30 minutes while the meatloaf cooks. The meatloaf is done when its internal temperature is 160°F, about 2 to 2½ hours.

4. Remove from the smoker to slice and serve immediately.

CAST-IRON CHILI

Instead of cooking chili all day on the stovetop or in a slow cooker, pop it into the electric smoker to give it a deep smoky flavor that's sure to make everyone happy. Slices of Easy Green Chile Cornbread (page 117) make the perfect accompaniment.

Prep time: 15 minutes   *Marinade time:* None   *Smoking time:* 2 hours

Wood chips: Hickory

Serves: 4 to 6

1½ pounds lean ground beef

2 (15-ounce) cans tricolored beans (or kidney or pinto beans), drained and rinsed

1 (15-ounce) can tomato sauce

2 cups water

3 tablespoons chili powder

3 tablespoons dried onion flakes

1½ tablespoons ground cumin

4 teaspoons coarse kosher salt

2 teaspoons dried minced garlic

1 teaspoon red pepper flakes

½ teaspoon cayenne pepper

½ teaspoon sugar

chopped white onions, grated cheese, and sour cream, as toppings

1. Prepare the smoker's water pan according to the manufacturer's instructions and preheat the electric smoker to 275°F. While it heats, fill a medium bowl with water and add 3 or 4 handfuls of hickory wood chips to soak.

2. Meanwhile, cook the ground beef in a large cast-iron pot on the stovetop over high heat. Stir and break the meat apart until it is crumbly and no longer pink. Drain off any fat liquid and add the beans, tomato sauce, water, and seasonings (chili powder through sugar). Stir well to combine and bring to a simmer.

3. Place the pot on the top rack of the smoker. Add a small handful of the soaked hickory chips to the chip loading area. Stir the chili and add more chips at least every 30 minutes. The chili is already fully cooked, but let it smoke for about 2 hours to let the flavors fully develop.

4. To serve, ladle the chili into bowls and top with chopped onions, cheese, and dollops of sour cream.

   Note: If your cast-iron pot has feet then it won't work on a flat-top stove. Use a separate stockpot to cook the chili mixture and then transfer to cast-iron pot before placing it in smoker.

HOMEMADE PASTRAMI

Homemade pastrami is a labor of love, but once you've made your own pastrami you'll never want store-bought again. I serve it on marble rye bread with a little Russian dressing, sauerkraut, and pickle spears.

Prep time: 30 minutes   *Brining time:* 5 to 7 days   *Smoking time:* 4 to 6 hours
Wood chips: Hickory
Serves: 10 to 12

FOR THE PICKLING SEASONING:

6 bay leaves, roughly crumbled

2 tablespoons mustard seed

2 tablespoons whole allspice

2 tablespoons whole coriander

2 tablespoons whole black peppercorns

1 tablespoon whole cloves

1 tablespoon red pepper flakes

1 cinnamon stick, broken in several pieces

TO PREPARE THE MEAT:

5 tablespoons Pickling Seasoning

1 cup plus 1 tablespoon light brown sugar, divided

1 cup coarse kosher salt

6 cloves garlic, smashed

1 onion, quartered

3 teaspoons pink curing salt (page 86)

1 gallon water

4 pounds beef brisket, fat trimmed

2 tablespoons black pepper

2 tablespoons paprika

¼ cup ground coriander

1 tablespoon garlic powder

1. Combine all the ingredients for the homemade pickling seasoning and store in an airtight container for up to 6 months.

2. In a 3 to 4-gallon container with a lid, combine the pickling seasoning, 1 cup brown sugar, kosher salt, garlic, onion, and pink salt with 1 gallon water. Stir well to combine and to dissolve the salt and sugar. Add the brisket and place a heavy bowl upside down on top of the meat to keep it submerged in the brine. Place the lid on the container and refrigerate for 5 to 7 days.

3. Prepare the smoker's water pan according to the manufacturer's instructions and preheat the smoker to 225°F. While it heats, fill a medium bowl with water and add 4 or 5 handfuls of hickory wood chips to soak.

4. Remove the brisket from the brine and rinse well under cool water for a couple minutes. The meat will feel denser and have a different texture and color than before it went into the brine. Dry with paper towels and set aside. In a small bowl, combine the black pepper, paprika, ground coriander, 1 tablespoon brown sugar, and garlic powder. Rub the mixture over the brisket to cover the entire surface with the seasonings.

5. Place the brisket in the smoker, fatty side up, and add a small handful of the soaked hickory chips to the chip loading area. Keep adding more chips at least every 30 minutes (or every 15 minutes, for a more intense smoke flavor). Smoke for 4 to 6 hours, or until the meat reaches an internal temperature of 165°F.

6. Remove from the smoker, wrap tightly in foil, and let sit for 2 hours. The meat will become even more tender as it sits. Thinly slice and store in an airtight container in the refrigerator for up to a week.

Notes: Brisket takes 1 to 1½ hours per pound to cook in the smoker. Start checking at the 4-hour mark to keep it from overcooking.

Pink Curing Salt

The pink salt used for curing meats such as bacon is a mixture of ordinary table salt and a small amount of sodium nitrite (and sometimes sodium nitrate, which turns into nitrite). Nitrites prevent the growth of bacteria and also enhance the meat's color and flavor.

This salt is dyed pink so that it's not accidentally used for other cooking, since nitrites aren't safe to consume in the amounts that regular salt gets used. When using pink salt, you need to rinse the marinated meat extremely well before cooking it, to make sure no pink salt remains on the meat.

You can find pink salt online or at outdoor/hunting stores. By the way, don't confuse pink curing salt with Himalayan pink salt—that's a naturally colored pure rock salt.

5 SEAFOOD

CAJUN SALMON BLTS

This sandwich was my husband's idea. After he went out to a local brewery for supper with his friends one night, he asked me to create a sandwich like the one he'd had there. I have to agree, it's delicious! It's just not complete without a huge smear of Smoked Walnut Pesto (page 105).

Prep time: 20 minutes   *Marinade time:* None   *Smoking time:* 30 to 40 minutes
Wood chips: Beech
Serves: 4

1 tablespoon onion powder

1 tablespoon paprika

2 teaspoons dried thyme

2 teaspoons garlic powder

2 teaspoons dried oregano

1 teaspoon coarse kosher salt

½ teaspoon cayenne pepper

½ teaspoon black pepper

⅓ cup mayonnaise

⅓ cup Smoked Walnut Pesto (page 105)

4 (4 to 6-ounce) salmon fillets, about 1 pound total weight (skin removed)

2 tablespoons olive oil

4 hearty rolls (such as ciabatta rolls)

8 slices hickory-smoked bacon, cooked

4 Romaine lettuce leaves

4 tomato slices

1. Prepare the smoker's water pan according to the manufacturer's instructions and preheat the smoker to 275°F. While it heats, fill a medium bowl with water and add 3 or 4 handfuls of beech wood chips to soak.

2. In a small bowl, combine the onion powder, paprika, thyme, garlic powder, oregano, salt, cayenne, and black pepper; set aside. In a separate bowl, combine the mayonnaise and the walnut pesto. Cover and refrigerate until ready to use.

3. Using paper towels, pat the salmon pieces dry. Rub each with a drizzle of olive oil and generously sprinkle with the dry seasoning mix. Store any leftover seasoning mix in an airtight container.

4. Prepare a foil pan by poking a dozen small holes in the bottom with a sharp knife and then lightly spraying it with cooking spray. The holes allow the smoke to penetrate the bottom of the fish without the need to flip the fish since it's delicate and might fall apart if flipped. Lay the fish in the pan and place in the smoker. Add a small handful of the soaked beech chips to the chip loading area, and keep adding more chips at least every 15 minutes. Smoke for 30 to 40 minutes, or until the thickest part of the fish reaches an internal temperature of 145°F.

5. Place each smoked salmon piece on a hearty roll generously spread with pesto mayonnaise. Top with 2 slices of bacon, a lettuce leaf, and a tomato slice.

BROWN SUGAR SALMON

The combination of brown sugar, maple syrup, and maple wood chips gives this salmon a slightly sweet flavor that's balanced nicely with the dill and mustard. This has become one of my family's go-to salmon recipes.

Prep time: 15 minutes   *Marinade time:* None   *Smoking time:* 1 to 1½ hours

Wood chips: Maple

Serves: 4

4 (6-ounce) salmon fillets, skin removed

2 tablespoons light brown sugar

½ teaspoon coarse kosher salt

½ teaspoon black pepper

zest of 1 large lemon

1 tablespoon chopped fresh dill

¼ cup real maple syrup

¼ cup yellow mustard

1. Prepare the smoker's water pan according to the manufacturer's instructions and preheat the smoker to 225°F. While it heats, fill a medium bowl with water and add 3 or 4 handfuls of maple wood chips to soak.

2. Check the salmon fillets for any small bones and place on a cutting board or tray. In a small bowl, combine the brown sugar, salt, and pepper. Rub the mixture over the tops and sides of the salmon fillets.

3. Transfer the fillets onto a large piece of parchment paper and carefully place in the smoker. Add a small handful of the soaked maple chips to the chip loading area, and keep adding more chips at least every 30 minutes.

4. While the salmon begins to smoke, prepare the maple glaze. In a small bowl, combine the lemon juice and zest, dill, maple syrup, and mustard, whisking to mix well. Brush the salmon with the glaze every 30 minutes.

5. Smoke for 1 to 1½ hours, or until the thickest part of the fish reaches an internal temperature of 145°F. Remove from the smoker and serve immediately.

JERK TILAPIA

After a trip to Turks and Caicos for my fortieth birthday, I couldn't stop thinking about the fish we'd had at a beachside restaurant called the Jerk Shack. There were so many layers of amazing flavors in that jerk fish, including an intense smokiness. I knew I had to recreate it in my smoker.

Prep time: 20 minutes   *Marinade time:* 30 minutes to 1 hour   *Smoking time:* 45 minutes
Wood chips: Pecan
Serves: 4

5 cloves garlic

1 small onion

3 jalapeño chiles, seeded (leave seeds to make it spicier)

3 teaspoons ground ginger

3 tablespoons light brown sugar

3 teaspoons dried thyme

2 teaspoons salt

2 teaspoons ground cinnamon

1 teaspoon black pepper

1 teaspoon ground allspice

¼ teaspoon cayenne pepper

4 (4 to 6-ounce) tilapia fillets

¼ cup olive oil

1 cup sliced carrots

1 bunch green onions, whole

2 tablespoons whole allspice

1. In a blender or food processor bowl, combine the first 11 ingredients (garlic through ground allspice) and purée well. Place the fish pieces in a large zip-top plastic bag, then add the puréed mixture and the olive oil. Seal and gently press the bag to coat the fish pieces with the marinade. Let marinate for 30 minutes to 1 hour in the refrigerator.

2. Prepare the smoker's water pan according to the manufacturer's instructions and preheat the smoker to 225°F. While it heats, fill a medium bowl with water and add 3 or 4 handfuls of pecan wood chips and the whole allspice to soak.

3. Prepare a 9 x 13-inch foil pan by poking a dozen small holes with a sharp knife in the bottom and spray with non-stick cooking spray. Spread the carrots and green onions across the bottom of the pan, arrange the fish pieces on top, and put the pan in the smoker. Add a small handful of the soaked pecan chips and allspice to the chip loading area, and keep adding more chips at least every 15 minutes. Smoke for 45 minutes, or until the temperature reaches 145°F in the thickest part of the fish.

Note: These fish fillets could also be smoked in individual foil pouches for easy serving. Just divide the vegetables onto 4 squares of foil, add the fish, and fold up the edges to seal. Poke about 6 small holes and smoke as directed above.

CUMIN-LIME SHRIMP SKEWERS

The bold flavors of smoky cumin and fresh lime zest are divine on these shrimp skewers. Just add a green salad for a light summer supper.

Prep time: 20 minutes   *Marinade time:* None   *Smoking time:* 30 minutes

Wood chips: Beech

Serves: 4 or 5

1 pound raw shrimp (31–40 size), peeled and deveined

8 wooden skewers

2 teaspoons coarse kosher salt

2 teaspoons ground cumin

2 teaspoons garlic powder

zest of 3 limes

1. Prepare the smoker's water pan according to the manufacturer's instructions and preheat the smoker to 275°F. While it heats, fill a medium bowl with water and add a handful of beech chips to soak.

2. Thread 5 or 6 shrimp onto each skewer and set aside. In a small bowl, combine the salt, cumin, garlic powder, and lime zest. Rub the mixture evenly over the shrimp.

3. Prepare a 9 x 13-inch foil pan by poking a dozen small holes with a sharp knife in the bottom and spray with cooking spray. Arrange the shrimp skewers in the pan and place in the smoker. Add a small handful of the soaked beech chips to the chip loading area, and add more chips after 15 minutes. Smoke for 30 minutes, or until the shrimp are fully cooked.

Tip: I often use raw frozen shrimp that have been deveined. Just let them thaw in the refrigerator for a few hours (or thaw under cool running water in a plastic bag), then peel and use as directed for whatever recipe you're making.

SEAFOOD SCAMPI

If you love shrimp scampi, then this smoked seafood version will blow your mind! A mix of shellfish is smoked in a garlic butter sauce, then tossed with pasta to create a rich seafood supper.

Prep time: 20 minutes   *Marinade time:* None   *Smoking time:* 30 to 40 minutes

Wood chips: Beech

Serves: 4

1 cup (2 sticks) butter

8 to 10 cloves garlic, finely minced

½ pound fresh scallops

½ pound crab meat

½ pound raw shrimp (31–40 size), peeled and deveined

pinch of salt

1 pound dry spaghetti or angel hair pasta

3 tablespoons finely chopped fresh parsley

1. Prepare the smoker's water pan according to the manufacturer's instructions and preheat the smoker to 275°F. While it heats, fill a medium bowl with water and add 3 or 4 handfuls of beech wood chips to soak.

2. In a small saucepan, gently warm the garlic and butter until melted. Alternatively, you can heat it in the microwave for 20 to 30 seconds in a microwave-safe bowl. Then pour the butter into an 8 x 12-inch foil pan. Add the garlic and a pinch of salt and stir to combine, then add the fresh seafood. Turn the seafood once or twice to coat with the garlic butter.

3. Place the pan in the smoker and add a small handful of the soaked beech chips to the chip loading area. Adding more chips at least every 15 minutes, smoke for 30 to 40 minutes, or until the seafood is fully cooked.

4. When the seafood is almost done, cook the pasta according to the package directions. Drain and toss with the smoked shellfish and garlic butter. Stir in the fresh parsley.

SIMPLE SEASONED CRAB LEGS

These crab legs were a happy accident. I was filling up the smoker for a giant Sunday supper, but I still had a little room in the smoker and I had a ton of crab legs left over from a party the night before. So I tossed them with lots of Old Bay and added them to the smoker. Some of the best things happen when I least expect them!

Prep time: 5 minutes   *Marinade time:* 10 minutes   *Smoking time:* 20 minutes

Wood chips: Beech

Serves: 4

1½ pounds precooked crab legs
(thawed if frozen)

¼ cup Old Bay Seasoning

melted butter, for serving

1. Prepare the smoker's water pan according to the manufacturer's instructions and preheat the smoker to 275°F. While it heats, fill a medium bowl with water and add 1 handful of beech wood chips to soak.

2. Place the crab legs in a 2-gallon zip-top plastic bag along with the Old Bay. Seal completely and shake vigorously to completely coat the crab legs. Let sit for at least 10 minutes to make sure the crabmeat is fully flavored with the seasoning.

3. Transfer the crab legs to a grill basket and place in the smoker. Add a small handful of the soaked beech chips to the smoker's chip loading area, and add more chips after 15 minutes. Smoke for 20 minutes, or until the crab is hot. Serve with melted butter for dipping.

6 SIDES

BACON

Making your own bacon is definitely a long process, but for any bacon lover it's something you have to try at least once. And I promise you, there's nothing better than the taste of your own homemade bacon!

Prep time: 15 minutes   *Curing time:* 7 days   *Smoking time:* 2 hours

Wood chips: Mesquite or hickory

Makes: about 2½ pounds bacon

4 pounds pork belly

¼ cup course kosher salt

¼ cup light brown sugar

5 cloves garlic, smashed

4 whole dried bay leaves

2 tablespoons coarse black pepper

2 teaspoons pink curing salt (page 86)

1. Cut the pork belly into 1-pound sections. Combine all the seasonings in a large bowl and mix well. Divide the seasoning blend into 4 portions and rub a portion over each pork belly, covering all areas well. Place each pork belly in a 1-gallon zip-top plastic bag. (Each belly needs its own separate bag, or it won't get enough seasoning and you'll end up with something that's more like Canadian bacon.) Refrigerate the bags for 1 week, turning them over daily and rubbing the meat through the plastic to make sure it's evenly covered with seasonings.

2. After 7 days, prepare the smoker's water pan according to the manufacturer's instructions and preheat the smoker to 200°F. While it heats, fill a medium bowl with water and add 3 or 4 handfuls of mesquite or hickory wood chips to soak.

3. Remove the pork pieces from the bags, rinse under cold water, and pat dry using paper towels. Arrange in the smoker with plenty of space around each piece, and add a handful of wood chips to the chip loading area. Smoke the pork for about 2 hours, or until it reaches an internal temperature of 150°F. The goal isn't to cook the bacon but to impart a strong smoke flavor, so keep the temperature low and the smoke level high. Add wood chips every 30 minutes.

4. Remove the bacon from the smoker and let cool. Then remove the remaining top layer of fat and slice the bacon as thick or thin as you like. Freeze any that you aren't going to use within a week, arranging the slices in a single layer in zip-top plastic freezer bags.

5. To use, cook the bacon as you normally would. I like to cook mine in a 425°F oven for about 20 minutes, or until crispy.

SMOKED WALNUT PESTO

Pesto is a great staple to keep on hand in your fridge. It can be used in so many ways besides being a terrific pasta sauce. Use it as a sandwich spread, add it to mayo to make a dip, or drizzle it over fish.

Prep time: 5 minutes   *Marinade time:* None   *Smoking time:* 1 hour

Wood chips: Maple

Serves: 4

1½ cups walnut pieces

⅓ cup grated Parmesan cheese

3 cloves garlic

1½ cups fresh basil leaves

1 teaspoon salt

⅓ to ½ cup olive oil

1. Preheat the smoker to 210°F without using the water pan. While it heats, fill a medium bowl with water and add 3 or 4 handfuls of maple wood chips to soak.

2. Spread the nuts in a disposable foil pan and place in the smoker. Add a small handful of the soaked maple chips to the chip loading area, and add more chips after 30 minutes. Stir the nuts every 15 minutes to be sure they smoke evenly for 1 hour.

3. Remove the walnuts from the smoker. When they've cooled, transfer them to the bowl of a food processor and pulse a couple of times. Add the Parmesan, garlic, basil, and salt and process a few times to chop and combine. When all the ingredients are finely chopped, slowly drizzle in ⅓ cup of the olive oil while the processor is running until incorporated. If the pesto seems too thick, drizzle in a little more oil.

4. Serve over pasta, or add to butter or mayonnaise to create a delicious topping. It's great on vegetables, potatoes, fish, and poultry. Store in an airtight container in the refrigerator for up to a week. Or freeze in a freezer-safe container for 2 to 3 months.

CAST-IRON BAKED BEANS

These beans are a classic barbecue side dish. Start with a couple cans of good ol' pork 'n' beans and you'll have a scrumptious side dish in no time.

Prep time: 5 minutes   *Marinade time:* None   *Cook time:* 1 hour

Wood chips: Any

Serves: 4

2 (31-ounce) cans pork and beans

8 slices bacon, cooked and roughly chopped, divided

¼ cup light brown sugar

½ cup Tangy Barbecue Sauce (page 12)

2 tablespoons Basic Barbecue Rub (page 14)

2 teaspoons Worcestershire sauce

1 jalapeño chile, halved and seeded (additional sliced jalapeño chile for serving, if desired)

1. Prepare the smoker's water pan according to the manufacturer's instructions and preheat the smoker to 275°F. While it heats, fill a medium bowl with water and add 3 or 4 handfuls of wood chips to soak.

2. In a 10-quart cast-iron pot, combine the beans, half of the cooked bacon, and all the remaining ingredients. Leaving the pot uncovered, place in the smoker and add a small handful of the soaked wood chips to the chip loading area. Adding more chips and stirring the beans at least every 15 minutes, smoke for about 1 hour. To serve, top with the remaining bacon and a couple jalapeño slices, if desired.

Smoking Veggies and Sides

I don't worry too much about what wood or temperature I use when I'm cooking a side dish such as baked beans, corn on the cob, or vegetables. I just put it in the smoker with whatever meat I'm cooking, at the appropriate amount of time before the meat is done.

CORN ON THE COB WITH SMOKED PESTO BUTTER

My mouth starts watering when I think about corn on the cob prepared in the smoker. I don't think there's an easier side dish. Of course, topping the corn with smoked pesto butter makes it a glorious treat.

Prep time: 20 minutes   *Soaking time:* 2 to 3 hours   *Smoking time:* 1 to 1½ hours

Wood chips: Any

Serves: 4

4 ears of corn, husks attached

1 cup coarse kosher salt

½ cup (1 stick) butter, softened

1½ tablespoons Smoked Walnut Pesto (page 105)

1. Prepare the corn by peeling back the husks and removing the silks, then pulling the husks back up over the corn. Fill a large bucket or a sink with cool water, add the salt, and stir to combine. Soak the corn in the salted water for 2 to 3 hours.

2. Prepare the smoker's water pan according to the manufacturer's instructions and preheat the smoker to 275°F. While it heats, fill a medium bowl with water and add 3 or 4 handfuls of chips to soak.

3. Remove the corn from the salt water, shaking off the excess. Place the ears directly on a smoker rack. Add a small handful of the soaked wood chips to the chip loading area, and keep adding more chips at least every 15 minutes. Smoke until tender, about 1 to 1½ hours.

4. Meanwhile, in a small bowl combine the butter and the Smoked Walnut Pesto, using a fork to blend them together. Set the pesto butter in the refrigerator to chill.

5. Remove the corn from the smoker. When it's cool enough to handle, remove the husks. Serve the corn with smoked pesto butter on the side.

SIMPLE SMOKED ASPARAGUS

Most vegetables can be smoked just like this asparagus, so if you aren't an asparagus fan, swap in your chosen vegetable. Try zucchini, yellow summer squash, carrots, or eggplant.

Prep time: 5 minutes   *Marinade time:* None   *Smoking time:* 1 to 1½ hours

Wood chips: Pecan

Serves: 4

1 bunch asparagus (about 1 pound), trimmed

2 tablespoons olive oil

1 teaspoon chopped garlic (about 2 cloves)

large pinch of coarse kosher salt

⅛ teaspoon black pepper

1. Prepare the smoker's water pan according to the manufacturer's instructions and preheat the smoker to 230°F. While it heats, fill a medium bowl with water and add 3 or 4 handfuls of pecan chips to soak.

2. Place the asparagus in a grill basket in a single layer. Drizzle olive oil over the top and sprinkle with the garlic, salt, and pepper. Toss gently to coat on all sides. Put the basket in the smoker and add a small handful of the soaked pecan chips to the chip loading area. Adding more chips at least every 20 minutes, cook for 1 to 1½ hours, or until the asparagus is just slightly tender but still has some bite to it.

MIXED VEGETABLE SKEWERS

Mix and match whatever vegetables you prefer to make this healthy side dish. Just make sure to cut all the vegetables the same size so they'll be done at the same time.

Prep time: 15 minutes   *Marinade time:* None   *Smoking time:* 1 to 1½ hours

Wood chips: Hickory

Makes: 10 skewers

2 zucchini, sliced in ½-inch rounds

2 yellow summer squash, sliced in ½-inch rounds

1 red onion, cut in large chunks

4 bell peppers (any color), seeded and cut in large chunks

1 pint (about 2 cups) container grape tomatoes

10 wooden skewers

2 tablespoons olive oil

2 tablespoons seasoned salt

1. Prepare the smoker's water pan according to the manufacturer's instructions and preheat the smoker to 250°F. While it heats, fill a medium bowl with water and add 3 or 4 handfuls of hickory chips to soak.

2. Thread the cut vegetables onto the skewers, alternating types and ending each skewer with a grape tomato. For easy handling, leave a couple inches on the dull end of the skewer free of vegetables. Drizzle on olive oil and sprinkle liberally with seasoned salt, making sure to coat all sides of the vegetables.

3. Arrange the skewers on the smoker racks and add a small handful of the soaked hickory chips to the chip loading area. Adding more chips at least every 20 minutes, cook for 1 to 1½ hours, or until the vegetables are just slightly tender but still have some bite to them.

SEASONED SPICY BROCCOLI

Don't let the name throw you—this broccoli isn't overly spicy, but it *is* flavorful. The red pepper just kicks it up a bit and makes this a little different than plain ol' broccoli. Broccoli is my kids' favorite vegetable, so it gets a lot of love at our house. I cook it almost the same way whether I'm using the smoker, the oven, or the grill. Each gives the broccoli its own unique flavor.

Prep time: 5 minutes   *Marinade time:* None   *Smoking time:* 1 to 1½ hours
Wood chips: Hickory
Serves: 4

1 head broccoli, trimmed and cut into florets

2 tablespoons olive oil

2 teaspoons seasoned salt

1 teaspoon red pepper flakes

1. Prepare the smoker's water pan according to the manufacturer's instructions and preheat the smoker to 230°F. While it heats, fill a medium bowl with water and add 3 or 4 handfuls of hickory chips to soak.

2. Place the broccoli in a grill basket in a single layer. Drizzle olive oil over the top and sprinkle with the seasoned salt and red pepper, then toss gently to coat.

3. Set the grill basket in the smoker and add a small handful of the soaked hickory chips to the chip loading area. Adding more chips at least every 20 minutes, cook for 1 to 1½ hours, or until the broccoli is just slightly tender but still has some bite to it.

EASY GREEN CHILE CORN BREAD

I love baking, but sometimes a mix is just easier than whipping out the measuring cups. Cornbread can be a little tricky, so go for the mix and doctor it up. Don't skip the mayonnaise—it keeps the cornbread super moist while it's smoking.

Prep time: 15 minutes   *Marinade time:* None   *Smoking time:* 1½ to 2 hours

Wood chips: Hickory

Serves: 4 to 6

1 (12-ounce) package cornbread mix

1 (4-ounce) can diced green chiles (hot or mild)

2 tablespoons mayonnaise

1. Prepare the smoker's water pan according to the manufacturer's instructions and preheat the smoker to 230°F. While it heats, fill a medium bowl with water and add 3 or 4 handfuls of hickory wood chips to soak.

2. Mix the cornbread according to the package instructions. Stir the chiles and mayonnaise into the batter.

3. Spray an 8-inch cast-iron skillet with cooking spray, coating it well. Pour the cornbread batter into the skillet and place in the smoker. Add a small handful of the soaked hickory chips to the chip loading area, and keep adding more chips at least every 20 to 30 minutes.

4. Smoke for 1½ to 2 hours, or until the cornbread is lightly browned and a toothpick inserted in the middle comes out clean. Cool slightly before serving.

7 DESSERTS

SMOKED NO-BAKE CHOCOLATE OATMEAL COCONUT COOKIES

My dad makes the best no-bake Chocolate Oatmeal Cookies every Christmas. I couldn't wait for Christmas this year and I really wanted a quick and easy cookie to make while smoking some ribs, so I created this smoked version of my dad's cookies.

Prep time: 20 minutes   *Marinade time:* None   *Smoking time:* 1 hour

Wood chips: Maple

Makes: 24 cookies

2½ cups quick-cooking rolled oats

1 cup sweetened flaked coconut

1 cup chopped nuts

2 cups sugar

6 tablespoons (¾ stick) butter

½ cup unsweetened cocoa powder

½ cup evaporated milk

1 teaspoon vanilla

1. Preheat the smoker to 210°F without using the water pan. While it heats, fill a medium bowl with water and add 1 or 2 handfuls of maple wood chips to soak.

2. Spread the oats, coconut, and nuts evenly in an 8 x 12-inch disposable foil pan. Place in the smoker and add a small handful of the soaked maple chips to the chip loading area. Add more chips at least every 15 to 30 minutes, and stir the oat mixture every 15 minutes so that everything smokes evenly. Remove from the smoker after 1 hour and let cool.

3. In a large stockpot, combine the sugar, butter, cocoa powder, and evaporated milk. Bring to a rolling boil on the stovetop over high heat and boil for exactly 1 minute. Remove from the heat and stir in the vanilla and the smoked oat mixture, combining well.

4. Drop the cookies by the spoonful onto wax or parchment paper. Let cool completely to firm up. Store in an airtight container at room temperature for up to one week.

SMOKED COCONUT MACAROONS

If you're a fan of coconut, you'll love these macaroons. The smokiness of the coconut adds an unexpected flavor that's almost addictive.

Prep time: 15 minutes   *Marinade time:* None   *Smoking time:* 1½ to 2 hours

Wood chips: Maple

Makes: 12 cookies

4 cups sweetened flaked coconut

4 egg whites

½ cup canned sweetened coconut milk

½ teaspoon vanilla

¼ cup sugar

1. Preheat the smoker to 210°F without using the water pan. While it heats, fill a medium bowl with water and add 3 or 4 handfuls of maple wood chips to soak.

2. Spread the coconut in an 8 x 12-inch disposable foil pan and place in the smoker. Add a small handful of the soaked maple chips to the chip loading area. Add more chips at least every 15 to 30 minutes, and stir the coconut every 15 minutes so that it smokes evenly. Remove from the smoker after 1 hour or when most of the coconut is golden brown and let cool.

3. Line 2 disposable 8 x 12-inch foil pans or small baking sheets with parchment paper; set aside. Turn up the smoker heat to 275°F.

4. In a large bowl, whisk the egg whites until frothy and add the smoked coconut, coconut milk, vanilla, and sugar. Stir well to combine. Drop by large tablespoonfuls onto the parchment paper. Place the pans in the smoker and add a small handful of chips to the chip loading area. Adding more wood chips at least every 20 minutes,

5. Smoke for 30 to 45 minutes, or until the cookies are lightly browned and the tops are set.

6. After cooling, store in an airtight container for up to one week.

SMOKED PEANUT BUTTER COOKIES

When I was testing these cookies, I took them to a family birthday supper at a well-known barbecue joint. The manager was walking by our table but stopped when he smelled the cookies, so I offered him one. He **oohed and** aahed about them, licked his fingers, and proclaimed that he wished he could put them on his menu!

Prep time: 15 minutes   *Marinade time:* None   *Smoking time:* 45 minutes to 1 hour

Wood chips: Maple

Makes: 12 cookies

1 cup peanut butter (crunchy or creamy)

1 cup sugar, plus more for the cookie tops

1 egg

1. Preheat the smoker to 275°F without using the water pan. While it heats, fill a medium bowl with water and add 1 or 2 handfuls of maple wood chips to soak. Line 2 disposable 8 x 12-inch foil pans with parchment paper and set aside.

2. In a medium bowl, combine the peanut butter, 1 cup sugar, and egg; mix well. Drop by tablespoonfuls onto the prepared pans. Dip a fork into sugar and press into the cookie tops twice, once in each direction, creating a crosshatch pattern.

3. Set the pans in the smoker and add a small handful of the soaked maple chips to the chip loading area. Adding more wood chips at least every 20 minutes, smoke for 45 minutes to 1 hour, or until the cookies are lightly browned and set on top. The cookies may still be a little soft, but they'll firm up as they cool.

4. After cooling completely, store in an airtight container at room temperature for up to one week.

   Note: The smoke flavor mellows out after a day or two, so eat these cookies right away in order to enjoy their full flavor.

CAST-IRON TRIPLE BERRY CRISP

I love making fruit crisps for dessert—they're so easy to put together and adaptable to whatever fruit I have on hand. I think this triple berry combination is my favorite. Just between you and me, I like to eat it for breakfast the next day, too.

Prep time: 5 minutes   *Marinade time:* None   *Smoking time:* 1½ to 2 hours

Wood chips: Cherry, apple, or maple

Serves: 6 to 8

2 cups (6 ounces) fresh blueberries

1 cup (6 ounces) fresh blackberries

1 pound fresh strawberries (about 2 cups)

½ cup light brown sugar

2½ tablespoons cornstarch

¾ cup all-purpose flour (regular or gluten-free)

¾ cup rolled oats

1½ cups granulated sugar

½ cup (1 stick) butter, cut in thin slices

1. Preheat the electric smoker to 275°F without using the water pan. While it heats, fill a medium bowl with water and add 2 to 3 handfuls of maple wood chips to soak. Spray a 10-inch cast-iron skillet with cooking spray.

2. Rinse the berries and spread on paper towels to dry. Cut the strawberries into pieces about the size of the blackberries. In a large bowl, gently combine the berries with the brown sugar and cornstarch. Pour into the prepared pan.

3. In another bowl, combine the flour, oats, and granulated sugar. Pour the mixture over the berries, making sure to completely cover them. The better everything is covered, the less likely the filling will bubble over. Scatter slices of butter all over the top of the oat mixture.

4. Place the pan in the smoker and add a small handful of the soaked maple chips to the chip loading area. Adding more chips at least every 20 minutes, smoke for 1½ to 2 hours, or until the top is lightly browned and crisp. Cool for 30 minutes before serving. Transfer any leftovers to a storage container, cover, and store in the refrigerator for up to one week

NO-CHURN SMOKED PEACH ICE CREAM

Nothing screams summer more than a big bowl of peach ice cream. Take it to the next level by using smoked peaches.

Prep time: 15 minutes   *Marinade time:* None   *Smoking time:* 1 hour   *Freezer time:* 4 to 6 hours

Wood chips: Maple

Serves: 6 to 8

4 peaches

1 (8-ounce) container unsweetened heavy whipping cream

1 (14-ounce) can sweetened condensed milk

2 teaspoons vanilla

1. Preheat the electric smoker to 210°F without using the water pan. While it heats, fill a medium bowl with water and add 3 or 4 handfuls of maple wood chips to soak. Prepare a 9 x 13-inch foil pan by poking a dozen small holes with a sharp knife in the bottom and spray it lightly with cooking spray. The slits will allow the smoke to come up through the bottom of the pan.

2. Cut the peaches in half, remove the pits, and place in the prepared pan. Set the pan in the smoker and add a small handful of the soaked maple chips to the chip loading area. Add more wood chips at least every 30 minutes. Remove the peaches from the smoker after 1 hour and let them cool completely, or refrigerate overnight.

3. Using a blender or food processor, purée the cooled peaches until nearly smooth, with just a few small chunks left. In a large chilled bowl, whip the heavy cream into stiff peaks and then gently fold in the sweetened condensed milk and vanilla with a spatula to keep the whipped cream from deflating. Gently fold in the peach purée until the peaches are almost fully incorporated—just a few large streaks of peach purée is ideal.

4. Pour into a metal bread pan and place in the freezer for 4 to 6 hours, or until frozen through. Serve within a couple days. Remove from the freezer a few minutes before serving; however, this ice cream will melt faster than store-bought ice cream, so don't let it sit out too long before serving it.

   Notes: Don't want to use heavy cream? Substitute with thawed frozen whipped topping, then proceed as directed.

EASY PINEAPPLE UPSIDE-DOWN CAKE

Here's a great way to use a boxed cake mix, and it couldn't be more delicious. Adding a dessert while your meat finishes cooking is a smart way to use your smoker.

Prep time: 15 minutes   *Marinade time:* None   *Smoking time:* 1½ to 2 hours

Wood chips: Pecan or maple

Serves: 8 to 10

1 (15.25-ounce) yellow cake mix or 2 (15-ounce) gluten-free yellow cake mixes

½ to ¾ cup light brown sugar

1 (20-ounce) can pineapple rings, drained

1 (10-ounce) jar pitted maraschino cherries, drained

1. Preheat the electric smoker to 225°F without the water pan. While it heats, fill a medium bowl with water and add 1 or 2 handfuls of pecan or maple wood chips to soak.

2. Prepare the cake batter according to the package instructions and set aside. Spray a 12-inch cast-iron skillet with cooking spray, coating well. Sprinkle the brown sugar into the bottom of the skillet to coat evenly. Arrange pineapple rings in a circle around the edge of the skillet and add another in the center. Place a cherry (without stem) in the center of each pineapple ring and add more cherries in between the rings. Carefully pour the prepared cake batter over the pineapple slices, being careful not to disturb the cherries.

3. Place the skillet in the smoker and add a small handful of the soaked pecan chips to the chip loading area. Add more wood chips at least every 20 to 30 minutes. Smoke for 1½ to 2 hours, or until the cake is lightly browned.

4. Remove the cake from the smoker and let it cool for 20 to 30 minutes. Run a butter knife around the inside edge of the skillet to loosen the cake. Then place a serving plate or cake stand upside down over the skillet and carefully invert the cake onto the plate. Serve warm or let cool for another 30 minutes to serve at room temperature.

Notes: Check to be sure a 12-inch skillet will fit in your smoker. If not, try a 9- or 10-inch skillet.

The smoke flavor will be more intense the second day if the cake is stored under a glass cake dome.

CONVERSION CHARTS

VOLUME CONVERSIONS

U.S.	U.S. Equivalent	Metric
1 tablespoon (3 teaspoons)	½ fluid ounce	15 milliliters
¼ cup	2 fluid ounces	60 milliliters
⅓ cup	3 fluid ounces	90 milliliters
½ cup	4 fluid ounces	120 milliliters
⅔ cup	5 fluid ounces	150 milliliters
¾ cup	6 fluid ounces	180 milliliters
1 cup	8 fluid ounces	240 milliliters
2 cups	16 fluid ounces	480 milliliters

WEIGHT CONVERSIONS

U.S.	Metric
½ ounce	15 grams
1 ounce	30 grams
2 ounces	60 grams
¼ pound	115 grams
⅓ pound	150 grams
½ pound	225 grams
¾ pound	350 grams
1 pound	450 grams

TEMPERATURE CONVERSIONS

Fahrenheit (°F)	Celsius (°C)	Fahrenheit (°F)	Celsius (°C)
70°F	20°C	220°F	105°C
100°F	40°C	240°F	115°C
120°F	50°C	260°F	125°C
130°F	55°C	280°F	140°C
140°F	60°C	300°F	150°C
150°F	65°C	325°F	165°C
160°F	70°C	350°F	175°C
170°F	75°C	375°F	190°C
180°F	80°C	400°F	200°C
190°F	90°C	425°F	220°C
200°F	95°C	450°F	230°C

RECIPE INDEX

ABOUT THE AUTHOR

Wendy O'Neal is the creator of the popular food and homemaking blog *Around My Family Table*. Her passion for sharing recipes and tips to help families gather around the supper table inspired her to begin the site in 2009. Wendy's award-winning recipes have been featured on numerous online sites, including the Huffington Post, BuzzFeed, FoxNews.com, MSN.com, Today.com, eHow, Epicurious, and many more. Wendy has also competed at the World Food Championships in the Food Blogger Division. Wendy's mom taught her to cook at an early age, but it wasn't until college and marriage to her high school sweetheart that she really found her love of cooking and developed her culinary skills. She taught herself how to grill and smoke shortly after she married, and since then she and her husband have had something going in the smoker almost every weekend. Wendy, her husband, and their two children live in Phoenix, Arizona. You can find Wendy at AroundMyFamilyTable.com, sharing her latest recipes, cooking tips, and homemaking ideas to help *your* family come together at the supper table.